Reflecting Rogue

First published by MFBooks Joburg, an imprint of
Jacana Media (Pty) Ltd
First and second impression 2017

10 Orange Street
Sunnyside
Auckland Park 2092
South Africa
+2711 628 3200
www.jacana.co.za

© Pumla Dineo Gqola, 2017
Cover photograph © Victor Dlamini Photography
Back cover photograph © Unathi Conjwa

All rights reserved.

ISBN 978-1-920601-87-4

Cover design by Shawn Paikin
Set in Sabon 11/15pt
Printed and bound by ABC Press, Cape Town
Job no. 003099

See a complete list of Jacana titles at www.jacana.co.za

Reflecting Rogue

Inside the mind of a feminist

Because feminist joy is fostered through rage + love.

Sisterly,
Pumla Dineo Gqola
06/04/2019
Berlin

Pumla Dineo Gqola

MF BOOKS JOBURG

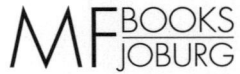

ALSO BY PUMLA DINEO GQOLA

What is Slavery to Me? Postcolonial/Slave Memory in Post-apartheid South Africa

A Renegade Called Simphiwe

Rape: A South African Nightmare

For
Bongi Mntambo
Neo Mntambo
Warona Ammar Nkosi
Kora Yakhisizwe Jennings

Contents

Reflecting rogue 1

Chapter 1: Growing into my body 5
Chapter 2: Battling to normalise freedom 13
Chapter 3: On the beauty of feminist rage 25
Chapter 4: Meeting Alice Walker 44
Chapter 5: Living like a girl 51
Chapter 6: When feminists fight 61
Chapter 7: A Blackwoman's journey through three South African universities 91
Chapter 8: A mothering feminist's life: A celebration, meditation and roll call 112
Chapter 9: When I grow up, I want to be me/you: Blackwomen, Joyful Struggle and the Academy .. 128
Chapter 10: Winnie, Wambui, Wangari – on being difficult women 145
Chapter 11: Writing African feminists: Celebrating FEMRITE at 20 158
Chapter 12: My mother's daughter, my sons' mother 177

Chapter 13: After Sobukwe: Time again for Africa's
           imagination 188
Chapter 14: A love letter to the Blackman who
           fathered me 201

Departures 208
Acknowledgements 211
Bibliography 213

Reflecting rogue

Writing is something I am almost always either doing or thinking about immersing myself in. It is here that I sit with myself and my thoughts, working them over, changing my mind, shifting how I feel about myself, a problem and the world. It is the place I am most often able to change my mind.

Yet, unlike many of my friends, I do not journal regularly, although I have diaries from when I was younger. Occasionally, the person whose thoughts I read about startles me. Sometimes it is that she is so young and different in how she sees the world to the person I have become. But I also always recognise a consistent core to those entries.

I remember the first day I knew I was a writer. The year was 1981. I was eight years old. My sisters and I had just changed out of the clothes we had worn to Mass and into clothes we could play in. But I could not immediately join Lebo and Vuyo, nor was I allowed to play with my baby brother Sizwe. Instead, I sat down to do the thing I hated most in the world, the thing I had been trying to perfect since before the short Easter break, the thing I was worst at but still had to do: memorising the recitation I would be required to perform in front of my Standard Two classmates the week schools reopened.

The teachers would only pick one of us, but we never knew

which one. I battled to focus, even with the fear of humiliation and caning for memory loss hanging over my head. So, I escaped, first, by translating the poem into another language, and later, carried away, I wrote a new poem. Because I was already a lover of words, this escape was joyful. Joyful escape is a kind of freedom.

I was already a reader, and it would seem a writer. Because words on a page have this effect on me, and even though I was supposed to be memorising the poem, the excitement drove me to share my distraction with my parents.

But it was my parents' reactions that transformed me from a mere escapist to a writer. Like many eight-year-olds, I was a show off who worshipped her parents. They treated those few lines like something spectacular, called me a poet. Of course, they had to explain that this new special word, "poet", was a writer of recitations. Although I would be much older before I realised that people could be jailed, killed or disappear for being much better writers, I had a taste that Sunday of the dance writing always has with power.

As I grew older, I realised that recognising the relationship between words and power was a complicated dance. Words wound and slay. Words raise and kiss. Words can be cage or springboard. In my life, they are both of these things so much of the day.

Today, writing is at the very centre of my life. It is where I love myself better. In my home, I have kept those journals from my teen years and thousands of other people's books, alongside the ones I write. Other people's books invited me into worlds and ways of being that would have been closed off to a little Blackgirl growing up in apartheid South Africa. They gave me better, freer ways to feel in my own skin, a community strange in the same ways I am, a bigger world to belong to.

My own writing is a compulsion. I write because it is the only way to fully be me.

Yet, writing is not always easy. Sometimes, it takes months to get an article or a short story or an essay just right. On other days, I am consumed and transported, staying in the zone until the sun sets and rises again. Knowing what I want to say and how I want to feel upon completion is not always helpful, and my relationship with deadlines is a rocky love-hate one. Once I never missed a deadline, and then, about a decade ago, this capacity slipped away.

Like my previous book, this offering has taken some turns away from what I planned when I embarked on this journey. It is my most personal book yet, but writing is always a risk. It is a lesson in letting go. What a paradox for writers, who are control freaks in so many ways. I pore over every sentence until I am either happy or defeated. Both are signs I need to let go and allow the writing to have its own life in the world.

Most of the chapters are new, even if they appeared in a much shorter version elsewhere. There are only two chapters that are unchanged, save for a different referencing style. The first was initially offered as the Robert Mangaliso Sobukwe 8th Annual Lecture. The second previously appeared in a collection on the experiences of Black South African women in the academy. I republish these here in an attempt to make them easier to find. They are the pieces of writing that I am most frequently asked to provide. Until now, it seems, they have been quite hard to find.

On 7 January 1997, I boarded a flight from Cape Town to Bloemfontein to take up my first full-time, adult job. That was twenty years ago, and as I hand over this collection, I am both very much still that determined young woman at heart, and softer, stronger and better. Many of the lives I set out to create for myself have been realised – through Grace, hard work, sacrifice, fire and love. Twenty years seems like a good time to bring together these essays in this form, but this is not a "best of".

These are reflections on country, self, family, community, pleasure, violence. It is a book nothing like my previous three. It is not on a subject – slavery, an artist, on rape. These are reflections of and on living, loving and thinking as feminist. One feminist.

CHAPTER 1

Growing into my body

I write and unwrite this chapter. Different versions of it lie on my floor with variously coloured handwritten notes in the margins. They are all fragments of how I think I want to talk about "my body", and, after writing and completing another piece, I realise that my resistance to writing this essay is linked to my desire to make it seamless, whole and smooth, to enable it to veil my anxieties about re-examining cuts and bruises. I am not sure how much of myself I want to expose and render vulnerable, and so, instead, I play games with myself. I want to mask the meeting points of purple and blue on skin that could either be tattooing or some other mark. It strikes me that embodied memories of pleasure are as far apart or as close together as we allow them to be. And it becomes clearer that this distance determines how we live the moments in between. So I offer no polished, stockinged or tweezed body of knowledge here. Rather, I wander through slides that offer fragments through which I read the landmarks of life's maze.

slide one: body language

> To remember something is an experience.
> — MARITA STURKEN

I am seven years old, sitting in a class in what has come to be called a typical black school. I do not know what's typical about anything really. There are seventy-six of us little people in desks that stand in rows from the front to the back, or from the door side to the window side, depending on how you choose to look at it. It is Religious Instruction period. Our teacher is a Blackman who told us last week, and the week before, and will tell us several more times, about how God likes fair-skinned people. This teacher will tell us about how fair-skinned is better, smarter, morally more developed. I am what he means by fair-skinned, as is he. Instead of feeling valued, I feel aggrieved for the people I love who would not be named fair-skinned.

I look back at this as an adult and I wonder what exactly it is that this teacher is telling us.

Is he telling us that *he* is all these things?

Is he exposing us to a world in which he is at the top of the hierarchy?

In this world, is *he* God? Is he recreating in front of his audience a world in which he is validated, not deviant, inferior, less than? Is this man, perhaps, also telling us about a planet on which we are stamped by white supremacy in ways that make us hate those who mirror us?

I am seven years old; it is 1980 in apartheid South Africa. I live in what I am later to learn is something that can be called "a remote part of the country" in a small town with much history. The history has pretty much chosen not to show itself as I sit at my desk. My teacher is not talking about a world in which white people are superior to Black people. This man is talking about gradations within Black society, within Blackness, between Black people, between who counts and who cannot. At this school I am to learn that the fair-skinned girls are prettier. Always. I am to learn that sometimes it occurs that darker-skinned boys or girls are beautiful too. These are sometimes called names like "coffee-coloured" or "dark beauties". I look around my class when my teacher tells us this for the umpteenth time and recognise that *we*, the children in my class, represent every shade of Black complexion that I am ever to know.

As an adult, I am struck by the frequency with which my mind conjures up this and other similar scenes. I know that my identity as a Blackwoman is not somatically determined, and that I am not a certain *kind* of Black person owing to the specific concentration of melanin in my skin. Yet the lingering memory suggests that this moment, and others like it, continue to play some role in my present, in my awareness of the competing, conflicting or connected ways in which my body can be read. It continues to haunt me, because I wonder what effects this brainwashing has on little psyches that are not exposed to alternative ways of viewing the world. I know that this teacher walked up and down rows of desks for close to four decades. I wonder when it became possible for us to teach ourselves, and our children, such intricate routes to hatred.

slide two: body image

A few years later I overhear an adult conversation. Many children know you are not supposed to eavesdrop. I had not mastered the art of disguising this exercise as described in Chris van Wyk's exquisite memoir. In his *Shirley, Goodness and Mercy* he suggests:
1. Don't sit quiet as a mouse. If you can hear them out there in the lounge, they can hear you here in the kitchen. And if you're quiet they know you're listening. Make busy noises like drinking a glass of water, sing bits from pop songs, calling to the dog outside. But don't overdo it.
2. Do something while you're listening. Read a book or some homework. If they come into the kitchen to switch on the kettle or something, they'll see a boy struggling with maths and not just staring at a wall.

3. Be wary of jokes coming from the lounge. If someone in the lounge tells a joke, try not to laugh. They'll know you've been listening all along.
4. If Ma calls you, don't answer immediately. If you do it's a dead giveaway and means you've had your ears tuned on them all the time.

Although my strategies for listening in on adult conversation are not as well thought out, I catch snippets of dialogue not intended for my little-girl ears, and I am careful not to be detected. One day I overhear the way in which a certain Blackman has had to cut off his dreadlocks in order to be able to assume a post he has been offered by the institution he wants to teach in, an institution in my proximity. I wonder what this means about hair; I wonder why this man's hair gets to be so unacceptable. Why a certain manner of wearing hair should be so important, so undesirable. I know my school has the same fascination with changing what is permitted: pretty plaits one year, and hair cut close to the scalp the next. I wonder why there are so many rules about what you can and cannot do with your own hair. I decide this is just bizarre adult behaviour.

Years later, as I grapple with different narratives, styles and hair-mories, I realise that this is troubled terrain. In a class I teach, a debate ensues about whether appearance can ever be a valid criterion for deciding on people's traits. This hurtles me further along the path of whether evaluations of bodies and appearance can ever be separated from discussions of race, gender and sexuality.

These are questions that shape our thinking on aesthetics. Beauty, we are told repeatedly, is skin deep. And yet we know that certain sizes and shapes, along with specific forms of body ornamentation, preening and pruning, count as beautiful. In contemporary South Africa we seem to be publicly experimenting, reinventing what counts as aesthetically pleasing, and beyond that, beautiful. This is an exciting process that we can, perhaps, participate in, because we have had to question so much about ourselves continuously.

slide three: body layering

I am thirteen years old, away at an all-girls boarding school in another part of the country. During communal ablutions (this is what the bathing is officially called here) we watch one another's movements and note differences in the way puberty affects our bodies. There are the intricacies of curvature simultaneously desired and feared: breasts grow fuller, hips assert themselves audaciously. Sometimes the routines of body care betray awkwardness with the unsuccessful concealment of evidence of menstrual blood. There are repeated discussions of the merits and demerits of sanitary towels versus tampons. Which pads are cooler and more comfortable: the clip-on, hook-on or stick-on ones? Do tampons really interfere with the hymen? And on it goes.

As teenagers are wont to be, we are acutely aware of similarities and differences within our midst. Regardless of our varied regions of origin we all take certain things for granted about the processes and art of hygiene. *Everybody* has two washing-cloths. One, preferably white, is to be used only on the face; the second, which is usually a deeper, richer colour, is allocated to washing "the body". The colours ensure that there is never confusion, never accidental contamination of the face by the dirty body. The dirtiness of the female body is "clear". We not only buy into this ideology of the dirty girl's body, we imagine that keeping the face, and sometimes torso, safe from the dirt of the bum, vagina and sometimes soiled feet is quite clever. We never wonder about how dirty our socked and shoed feet are. We are quite clever, by extension, for absorbing this discipline which we know *somehow* requires mastering as part of our entry into ladyhood. Cleverness and hygiene seem to merge into some uncanny union, even for those labelled as "tomboys".

Later we were to ask questions about the pervasiveness of notions of purity and contamination in our relationships with ourselves. When I ask friends and relatives about the washing-cloths midway through writing this piece, it emerges that the tyranny of the two washing-cloths is not central to adult femininities. This is not to say that by adulthood we have all mystically freed ourselves from notions of purity and impurity. The pages of women's magazines world-wide continue to extol the virtues of products necessary to conceal, disguise and rein in unruly female body smells, shapes and protrusions. Therefore, whereas the religion of Blackgirl hygiene stressed the separation of face and body washing-cloths, followed by the obligatory washing of our panties, as adult women the regimens of body cleansing include numerous products to ensure control of the body's textures, smells and shapes.

Patricia McFadden has argued that this obsessive narration of women's bodies in terms of their assumed impurity and being out-of-control is linked to the fear of thinking about women's bodies in relation to pleasure and/or power. These notions of containment of the girl-and-later-woman's body are linked to other ways of living in and through our bodies. It cannot be detached from other messages communicated to us as we are socialised into thinking of our bodies as burdens and our minds or souls as the only chance we have of transcending the mire of the bodies we drag with us. Again, I wonder why it is so important to teach hatred of self as a primary emotion through which to negotiate our existence on this planet.

embracing alternatives

I never believed my teacher, even as a child. I knew that the intelligent people in my family like my sister and father, the devout ones like my Nkgono, the ones I relished in observing like Mam'Nambi, were not uniform in skin tone. I recognised that the boy who was my friend, Fika, with whom I competed for first position, was not stupid, no matter what this teacher said. I was struck by too many obvious contradictions in my family, in my friendships, in my world. There were also teachers in the same school who taught explicitly and through example that life was full of possibilities, that a questioning mind was always an asset and that you could still enjoy your body. It helped that my parents were invested in the same project as these perceptive teachers.

The previous body recollections strike me as linked to efforts to make us distance our spiritual and mental selves from the ways in which we are embodied. Of course, these saturate the world beyond the specific spaces within the Black society that I grew up in in the seventies and eighties. We have all been irritated by the barrage of chain blond jokes at parties, in our email inboxes, and elsewhere. From different angles we are bombarded by such ideologies: in institutionalised religion, various philosophical and other intellectual traditions, and through the assorted popular cultural forms we participate in molding. These messages safeguard the separation of the body from the more abstract entity altogether: mind and/or spirit. In the binary oppositional way we have been programmed to think, and often continue to be complicit with, this means one is good and the other bad. They cannot just be different. And so generation after generation we are told we have to choose: either efface our bodies when in pursuit of cerebral interest or highlight the aesthetically approved body.

dancing between the masks

> In your sure-footed stride
> across troubles and joys
> do your steps ever falter?
> – Abena PA Busia

I no longer choose. The metaphor and visual representation of dancing between masks speaks to me. In the Thembinkosi Goniwe print of the same name, I am intrigued by the joy on the faces of those dancing. It has become important to realise that the activity between these two masked positions, body and intellect, is not just struggle. You can dance there. And, yes, there are "troubles and joys".

It is crucial to begin to make new memories of embodiment: forms that encourage pleasure and power. Running with the dancing and sure-footed metaphors, we touch the space where body and mind/

spirit perform not as competitors but as playmates. And it should be possible to continue to think critically and *insurgently* about what play means sexually, politically, spiritually and any-other-ly. Enjoying the play, and making it our home, cannot be trapped in conventional beauty and acceptability when these are designed to make us disappear: nip, tuck, tweeze, wax, cover, starve, bleach.

Today, I am an adult woman. My agency exists even in the face of powerful institutionalised forms of violence. To assert this insurrectionary agency, to speak as a feminist rogue, disloyal and disrespectful of the rules of patriarchy, as a teacher, as an older Blackwoman, is my responsibility and, I imagine, one we all should share. Today my spirit-mind-body-self delights, frightens, pleasures, shocks and is. My body is the home of my spirit – not its temple – and I like the shiny dip on one shin from when my leg caught on a rusty nail as I rushed back to my seat before the teacher returned to her classroom, the scratches here and there from losing balance as I climbed a wall or tree, the adventurous strand of hair there, and even the protruding bone on my foot that makes it hard for me to wear certain shoes. My spirit is the oil and incense in my body and I relish its textures, its slipperiness and its fire, even as I am aware of its explosions. It excites me to think that in some small way I contribute daily to the uncovering of possibilities for children and younger people. I see signs that there are people engaged in this every day, especially today at the bottom of this amazing continent I was made from. As I walk the streets of the cities and small towns of this southern region, I am delighted by the creative ways in which people are engaging with their bodies more and more. There is a tickle in my spirit-place when I see young Blackwomen, especially, communicating comfort and love of themselves to themselves. It is a wonderful energy, because it confirms to me the chain reaction we set off when we allow ourselves to become an expression of who we really are, and can be.

CHAPTER 2

Battling to normalise freedom

I was born in December 1972, and so that makes me a child deeply shaped by the cultures of the 1970s and '80s, as I moved through childhood. It also means that I was 21 when I voted for the first time in 1994.

When I speak to my students, and to some young people, whose childhood was in the 1990s and the 2000s, I recognise the incomprehension of how hopeful 1994 was, what a relief to have an opportunity to think of ourselves differently than we had under apartheid. It may be a gap that is simply impossible to bridge in comprehension. And that gap makes post-apartheid failures so devastating, not because nothing has changed – for this is simply not true – but because too little has changed in ways that expand the vision of what is possible, and too much has changed in directions that should have remained unrealisable. Everywhere, and increasingly, there are reminders of missed opportunities to create the country we dreamt of as I entered adulthood.

I borrow the phrase of normalising freedom from Njabulo Ndebele, writer, cultural theorist and leading academic, who uses it to express the move away from simply gaining freedom to being able to fully experience the range of what freedom means. Ndebele coins the phrase "the difficult task of normalising freedom" for the new South Africa: political freedom was achieved and yet this achievement continues to be contaminated by – and intertwined with – various continuing forms of unfreedom: economic marginalisation, gender-based violence (within which I include homophobic violence), as well as the ascendance of newer forms of policing and surveillance.

In the lead up to 27 April 1994, the African National Congress election campaign material included a poster of smiling Nelson Mandela in a black, brown and gold shirt surrounded by children of different skin and hair colours, themselves clothed in vibrant colours. The shirt was in the style of what would later be known as the Madiba shirt. The children around him look relaxed and some have the recognisably strained "photo smile" that many young children often adopt. A green banner with white writing at the top promises "A better life for all". Running horizontally across the bottom are four squares, one each for the letters ANC, the ANC flag, a passport photograph of a smiling Mandela in dark jacket, white shirt and grey tie, and a giant X. The bottom is a strip from an election ballot.

Each time we saw it in 1994, we knew it was a poster selling a dream we had waited too long to see materialised. However, it was also a poster that spoke without irony in the specific race language we were invited to vote ourselves away from. It looked like one of those billboards, posters and magazine adverts for United Colours of Benetton: a range of people with different skin tones and other signifiers of race clad in colourful clothing, arranged so that their bodies touched slightly, against a white backdrop. The most important message in those ubiquitous Benetton print advertisements, as in the "A better life for all" advert, appeared uncluttered in white font on crisp green background. The poster represented "all" through visual markers of difference that suggested embodied race classification. Yet, at the time, the promise in the poster made little sense when materiality was considered. How could the lives of white beneficiaries of apartheid be (further) improved, rendered "better" under a post-apartheid ANC-led government?

The slogan seemed partly informed by the tensions and fears of Black retribution, the spectre of swartgevaar had been one of the cornerstones of apartheid narrative. Such a slogan could allay white voters' fear of Black people; assure them that Black people would not kill them in their sleep and confiscate their property once in power.

The poster connected voting for the ANC to creating a better life for all South Africans. The banners visually frame the smiling, reconciliatory Mandela – eliding the terrorist Mandela around whom swaartgevaar coalesced and absenting Mandela the beloved revolutionary on the island. Yet, for most Black voters, it was the revolutionary Mandela we placed our faith in, and wanted to see as President. Remembering a past not too long ago when he was deemed the most dangerous man to apartheid South Africa, so dangerous that just saying his name was criminalised, and his photograph unpublishable, we relished the idea of voting for our terrorist president in the bright light of day. As his pictures were suddenly everywhere from 1990 onwards, I remembered the excitement I had felt with a few schoolmates in 1986 on our way to our boarding school, Inanda Seminary, when a Durban newspaper had flouted legal restriction and published his image on the front page. The excitement resided in knowing how dangerous having access to that shared copy was, before the Special Branch had managed to confiscate and ban all copies. We sat huddled around that image, imagining that he still looked like he had when the picture had been taken. A group of teenagers huddled around a newspaper page trying to memorise his face. I realise now that I failed dismally at that task, and it could have been a photo of anybody really.

Nonetheless, the possibility of Mandela, the mysterious uber-revolutionary superhero of our childhood, as President of our country was so intoxicating that we imagined all the questions being raised about the televised negotiation process, about the Convention for a Democratic South Africa (CODESA) and other aspects of the nation-anticipated, by those less trusting of the ANC, would be resolved under a new government.

Gazing at this poster, these memories and desires were projected onto the central figure. However, this is not what the poster suggests. Rather, the Mandela of the election poster is a grandfather Mandela. His much-cited longing for children's voices and the sight of children while incarcerated is suggested in the poster's image. That is the only link – and a very tenuous one – to his imprisonment evoked in the poster. In other words, we can remember his prison experience only for the longing he had for children, his own and others. The poster is his promised delivery from this decades-long yearning. However, the metaphor does not hold. He cannot be compensated for the loss of time with his children, as individual narratives from his various children will remind us before and after we vote.

Yet both Mandela as terrorist and revolutionary Mandela are remembered by different segments of the electorate; some just have to work harder to hold on to an image of Mandela that resonates. The contrast between the grey, smiling Mandela and the bright-eyed children also speaks to a future.

If children are the face of the new South Africa that we had to imagine in early 1994, the relationship to our past was not entirely clear. We had to think of *race as colour* (superficial difference) but not of *race as power* (i.e., the racism of the past and present). In other words, the invitation to Black audiences was one of escape, a counterintuitive one. However, wanting to escape from apartheid was something radical movements had long taught us to do. We grew up on the slogan "freedom in our lifetime", even though everywhere around us was evidence of the power of a brutal apartheid state. Indeed, what made it possible for the oppositional slogans "each one teach one" and "freedom before education" to co-exist in the 1980s was this capacity to imagine the impossible as inevitable. To even entertain, as a young Black person under apartheid, that freedom was so urgent that it would arrive in your youth provided you gave the struggle your all. That you would still have time for education after was immersion in the counterintuitive. In my late twenties, a chosen family member, himself Caribbean and Black British, would ask me how it was possible to live through apartheid and keep pushing through. Coming from a person whose life's work is humanising enslaved and indentured people from previous centuries, rendering their contribution to British and global culture visible, it was a hard question. In some senses, he knew the answer. In another, telling him we heard "freedom in our lifetime" so much that we believed it was Greek to him. It was counterintuitive given what he knew about the power of the apartheid state and its allies in Reagan's America, Thatcher's Britain, Israel and the dishonest European banks that bankrolled Pretoria.

So, when the poster invited us to make an imaginative leap, this was an exercise we were so accustomed to, we missed how the ends had shifted. The future suggested in the poster is not a post-race, post-patriarchal, post-capitalist one. It is an innocent future that matters, a co-created future that rests on innocence, innocence from racism as institutional violence too, which is to say an invisibilisation of racism. The poster suggests a future where quality of life transcends *race as power*, even as it evokes *race as colour* in its visual vocabulary.

The "better life" rests on the bright faces of the children around Mandela and on the voters prioritising them and the future, muting the past. It requires that we believe a future free of institutionalised white supremacy is possible if we vote ANC, and in that moment it still is. It is discursively compelling and visually arresting. But many of us will vote for revolutionary Mandela because of the very past and present of white supremacist wounding that the poster avoids. Our memory will exceed the call to aspiration. We will take the imaginative leap that we are well-trained in biographically, and that has been a crucial part of being Black in the world, transmitted across generations; enabling us to survive slavery, genocide, conquest and now, at last, apartheid.

That was March 1994.

I wrote the first, shorter version of this chapter in March 2015, a few weeks away from the anniversary of the first South African election. I fleshed it out two years later for inclusion in this book. Anniversaries are not just cause for celebration; they can also be moments to pause and reflect. I was twenty-one years old, four months into my second degree when I voted in 1994. Much ink has been spilt on what this moment meant for many who could vote legally for the first time. The snaking voting queues have become as iconic as pictures of Mandela with children, beyond that first one. We have been told repeatedly of how virtually no violent crimes were reported on that day and we imagine optimistically that none were committed that day. Given the constant onslaught that apartheid was on the body and psyche, and with these kinds of narratives and visual prompts, it is understandable why aspirational tags such as the "miracle" or "dream" transition gained currency.

> Escape.
> Newness.
> Relief.
> Possibility.

Even as I revise the chapter extensively in April 2017 – sceptical of the vision on that poster, aware of how prophetic its most dangerous promise was, having barely mentally survived the brutality with which #RhodesMustFall and #FeesMustFall were met – still, with heart and head overflowing with disillusionment at contemporary South Africa's devastating Black poverty and maddening misogynist violence, there is a little spark of nostalgia for 1994; for what we could have been, for what we hoped for. It is a devastating awareness, this living memory for who we were in April 1994.

> Hope.

Rising to the occasion, Archbishop Desmond Tutu would dub us "the rainbow children of God", in a phrase I have revised my stance on many times since the 1990s. Initially raging against it as obscuring race by reducing it to mere difference without hierarchy, I have come to wonder, after Gayatri Spivak's work on how the centre mutates and appropriates radical critique in order to sustain itself, about whether it is not useful to distinguish between what Tutu coined and how it moved into the mainstream parlance.

Given Tutu's consistent opposition to apartheid terror, his treatment by the apartheid state as a dangerous person, why is it so hard to imagine that Tutu was referencing rainbow as exists in global Black thought? What if it is not Tutu's formulation but its appropriation into rainbowist nationalism that is dangerous? When Ntozake Shange, African American feminist poet, essayist, activist and novelist, wrote the iconic choreopoem *For colored girls who have considered suicide when the rainbow was enuf*, a text that remains a global Black feminist classic several decades on, "rainbow" was not avoidance of race, difference and the violence of hierarchy. It was a direct confrontation of violent hierarchy, an attempt to imagine how difference might work for a decolonial project of recognition. When the LGBTI movement embraces rainbow metaphorically, it is a gesture that refuses co-option, erasure and a deliberate political move to try to make difference link with freedom rather than annihilation. Jesse Jackson's Rainbow Coalition emerged out of an unapologetic civil rights investment, confronting rather than avoiding difference, and attempting to create a world in which difference was not divisive. It is an ambitious project.

Tutu's biography suggests that he was gesturing intertextually to these diverse traditions of investing rainbow with meaning. However, he did not have full control over how that concept would travel. Increasingly, I wonder whether Tutu's rainbow is an attempt at remaking, not avoidance or flattening of difference. He has remained a most troublesome figure for the project of rainbowism – seeming to be its biggest proponent in giving it a language, and heading its most powerful instrument, the Truth and Reconciliation Commission (TRC), but also constantly undermining the premises of the rainbow nation: its gender power, its deepening poverty, its violent masculinist leaders, corruption, criticising not only the easy-to-fault presidents, but Mandela too on a few counts. He repeatedly breaks rank to endorse reproductive choice and same-sex marriage, in ways that complicate his position as (retired) Archbishop. His refusal to hold his tongue post-apartheid is why he was derisively dubbed "Deputy Jesus" by former South African Commissioner of Police Bheki Cele. On a lighter note, I have often wondered whether it is not the exact task of an Archbishop to (aspire to) be even more like Jesus than ordinary Christians.

Regardless of what Tutu intended by "rainbow nation", its absorption into post-apartheid nationalism flattened the hierarchy and institutional violence encoded in difference, instead of transforming it. Later still, we would be invited to aspire to "unity in diversity". Unity has always been a double-edged sword for the marginalised, and the transformation of the "rainbow" into "unity in diversity" cemented the avoidance of difference, the deferral of justice for apartheid's victims. And apartheid's victims were not just those who fell into the narrow category defined by the TRC. Violence victimises its targets. Black people may be survivors, but they were also apartheid's victims.

Not all of us were euphoric in the 1990s. Indeed, even as we voted on 27 April 1994, many Black people deliberately withheld their votes in painful, principled refusal to accept the negotiated settlement. At the risk of being seen as the misguided renegades who would not come to the celebratory table, they insisted that real power was not transferring hands, that too much had been compromised at the negotiating table, that the nightmare that was apartheid would continue in a different guise. They resisted the nation mythmaking, they kept their eyes firmly on *race as power* and rejected *race as colour* as alibi for injustice.

I remember how much tension there was in many families, how devastating it was to see the low Pan Africanist Congress (PAC) showing at the polls even as many PAC members had publicly announced they would not participate. To watch the uncontested ANC wins in PAC strongholds, to see the even lower polling of Azanian People's Organization (AZAPO), mixed some bile into the results of that first election for many of us, even if these were not parties we chose to vote for.

Many years later some of these renegades' children, along with many children of willing voters, "born-frees", deferred their own first vote. Race, racism and the state of Black life, had everything to do with this refusal on both counts. It is unsurprising that the refusal to vote by increasing numbers of eligible South Africans is readily dismissed across media and political parties as "apathy" or the "sign of a maturing democracy" resonant with voting patterns in some global North countries. This too is a refusal to confront the failure of the reconciliation myth, of unity in diversity and of rainbowism.

In the Black public sphere, public intellectuals had long dubbed the national narrative "reCONciliation". Lizeka Mda and Christine Qunta published remarkably similar critiques of the violence and injustice of the reconciliation and rainbow nation motifs in 1996. Several senior Black journalists (many of whom have subsequently changed course) received tongue-lashings from then Deputy President Thabo Mbeki for their critical distance from the official narrative, and many did not mince their words in response to him in various editorials as well as on the pages of *Tribute*. Later in the same decade, Xolela Mangcu cautioned against the projection of apartheid racism on generals, colonels and select politicians, reminding us of the everydayness of racial violence under apartheid. Such insistences on taking *race as power* were as unfashionable in media and academia then as they are today.

Yet, fashionable or not, these rejections of nationalist narratives explain why we have a society that seems further away from "A better life for all" in 2017 than it did in 1997. This glossing over difference rather than systemic change has emboldened the worst kinds of violence. This is why we have constant explosions of naked racism now, why Helen Zille, an opposition party leader, can make an argument for the gains of colonialism. This is what the last two decades have enabled by negating the need for accountability, atonement and justice: racial harassment has moved from the hidden or individual to brazen articulation in public spaces, while Black poverty remains transmitted across generations.

The early detractors from the rainbow nation mythology

underlined the value of linking race to justice as the way to undo the legacy of race. They required an interrogation of white power, recognising that pontificating on the social constructedness of race does not mitigate white supremacist violence. Such statements about constructedness very often invisibilise racism, stressing the need to focus on accent and nuance at the expense of pattern.

Today, it is not hard to recognise that rather than transcend race, white supremacist violence is gaining ground. Knowing that race is not "real" is no protection against racial harassment and extreme violence. White epistemic and economic power is entrenched in the economy, land ownership, language dominance and the academy. I have been in meetings where colleagues voiced the kind of naked white supremacist statements that they would have disguised a decade ago, where colleagues laughed as someone spoke of the bludgeoned, shot at, displaced bodies of student activists on our campus, where colleagues who previously argued against all forms of violence insisted that militarised campuses, tear gas canisters thrown into teaching and administrative buildings, and bullet wounds on our students' bodies were unavoidable, and necessary to ensure that, unlike the University of Cape Town, our academic calendar concluded in December 2016.

Outside of government, the most powerful institutions in corporate and higher education have remained stubbornly resistant to transformation of culture or numbers.

The return of white supremacist violence to the sphere of the spectacular is everywhere evident from the resurgence of older notions of race, once again taking a grip on the popular imagination. The peers of the children around Mandela continue to live highly raced lives. Their race and inherited class position is more likely to determine whether they can afford school fees and are able to graduate, than their aptitude. Each challenge to how race works to exclude in the academy is met with statistics that show that university undergraduate enrolments are demographically representative. But this information is deceptive. The real answer lies in the demographics of who graduates, when, and with(out) student debt.

Every year we lose some of our best students because of inability to afford education. For many years, academics have complained of students passing out in class, sleeping in libraries, under stairs and "squatting" in friends' rooms, of students who live on popcorn because it is filling and the only thing they can afford. The private food vendors on campus make food unaffordable. Some of the people I was a student with in the 1990s at UCT have no idea how different and unaffordable campus life is. They assume that our students' residence fees include all meals, as ours did and that the university offers a range of affordable food options in canteens. These are the many ways in which race continues to matter. Students who travel for three hours on public transport to attend an eight o'clock class are more likely to be Black and poor/working class than not. At their most brilliant, they remain at a distinct disadvantage. This is not "just" class at play. It is not just the legacy of apartheid. It is the failure to create a different society with opportunities to be free of poverty. Students in my first year class in 2017 were born in the second year of democracy. They are younger than the children around Mandela on the poster I started with.

Avoiding race power has led not to the disappearance but to emboldened racism – institutional and individual.

A group of young white men who were either babies or not yet born in 1994 forced Black labourers to consume urine on camera at an institution of higher learning in the Free State, while another group at the same institution assaulted a Black fellow student a few months later. At a different institution in the Northern Cape, white students raped a Black student who has a white mother.

Closer to home, teachers separate students into Black groups and white groups for teaching in a school in Gauteng; Black parents have to go to court to force transformation of the governing body at an Eastern Cape private school and to ensure the teaching of isiXhosa at the same institution.

At Wits University, the campus newspaper reports that young white women racially harassed and threatened to assault a student who questioned their mocking of a Black academic's pronunciation.

In the Western Cape a domestic worker is assaulted in the suburb in which she works because the white man who assaults her "mistakes her for a prostitute" and "snapped [...] as a result of having these people in our area".

Perhaps the neighbourhood-watch crew that has issued labourers in one suburb with green access cards in order to keep out those who do not belong there has the same idea. In the same province, a vice chancellor of a prestigious South African university defends his institution's failure to hire significant numbers of Black staff and its negligible numbers of senior Black academics through statements so baffling it is not clear how they are to elicit sympathy for the institutional choices. "We" had one African woman professor two years ago but she left. It takes an average of twenty years from PhD to full professorship. "We" are not the only ones.

It is an exhausting list even as it is the proverbial tip of the iceberg. The dream of a miraculous democracy has turned into a nightmare. It is unlikely to be moved by the rhetoric of social construction, ubuntu and further mythologisation of diversity under the guise of *race as colour*. In the official public political sphere, we are beginning to see the emergence of a new grammar of resisting racial terror, one that disrespects the regimented conventions of academic and parliamentary protocol. As one "born-free", Model C educated, Black radical with two Wits degrees pointed out in a conversation on everyday racism and investor confidence recently "if the country has to collapse first for us to own it, then so be it. It may be a mess we need to build from scratch, but let it be." Another similarly located Black radical challenged "you keep telling us that we are worlds away from apartheid, so tell those of us who were not alive in the '70s and '80s, how is it different? Why are you not angrier?"

It is a good question.

CHAPTER 3

On the beauty of feminist rage

Every August, millions of South Africans move collectively in a carefully choreographed dance called Women's Month. For almost five dizzying weeks, women are praised, patriarchy decried and women's gains celebrated. There are awards ceremonies, gala dinners and public service announcements. Inspired by the courageous coordinated efforts of savvy women who organised the march to the Union Buildings to protest against the extension of passes to African women in 1956, each August we recall their names and marvel at their achievements. We catch our collective breath to take stock of how far we have come, and to reflect on how rocky the ground beneath our feet remains. Sometimes we re-enact the march as spectacular and miraculous; stirred by how twenty-thousand women could organise across class, geographic and race barriers such a feat at a time before cellphones and social media.

Even as we marvel at the women led by Sophia Williams-de Bruyn, Rahima Moosa, Lilian Ngoyi and Helen Joseph, we pretend they represent a moment, rather than sophisticated movement building. History has airbrushed the other successful women's marches that predated 9 August 1956 out of view. Women's world-changing collective political organising is inconvenient to national history. Yet, the memory of this march stands as a reminder of this legacy of intergenerational, bold women's activism and power to galvanise against a powerful apartheid state in ways not easy to explain or co-opt into a masculine narrative of heroic nationalism that would usher in a new dispensation.

Today, and increasingly these days, I find myself turning to June Jordan, Jamaican-American feminist, essayist, activist. I re-read her poem first read in 1978, and first published in 1980 titled 'Poem for South African women'. It is in that poem that she declared "we are the ones we have been waiting for" as her closing line.

The poem is about the power of bold, collective imagination, which stands defiantly in the larger context of individual fear, personal shadows and need for clarity. In it, Jordan writes the women's collective action as a way to overcome individual limitation, and to band together to make a new earth. Quite literally, in the third to sixth lines, the women's thousands of feet "pound the fallow land/into new dust that/rising like a marvellous pollen will be/fertile". In the stanza that follows, what these women create through their "ferocious affirmation/of all peaceable and loving amplitude" is certainty for a different future that has become "irreversible" by the end of the third stanza. The fourth and final stanzas read:

> And who will join this standing up
> and the ones who stood without sweet company
> will sing and sing
> back into the mountains and
> if necessary
> even under the sea
>
> *we are the ones we have been waiting for.*

In this poem, then, June Jordan projects forwards the enormous impact this march will continue to have, even as she is aware that it did not technically succeed in stopping the extension of Pass Laws to African women under apartheid. The optimism, celebration and commemoration in the poem, then, are not about the immediate success of the direct course of action. Rather, when the women's action changes the world, this gestures to the many other successes we continue to reap from the collective action of those women more than sixty years ago.

It seems impossible to imagine that under such repressive times and surveillance, women could organise repeatedly and refine a model of organising that worked to mobilise across class, race, geography, religion, transgress the boundaries of who was directly affected and who not, and in coordinated action speak in one voice. In Jordan's poem and for many of us, the march was not about glossing over differences. Nor was it about transcending differences. Those women activists knew the value of working in different organisations – church, union, organisational, social – and many came from sites that were not non-racial or multi-racial. Some of them came from organisations that had a single class, or were only Black or only white women's organisations. Some came from black, Indian and coloured only groupings. They understood something profound about organisation and movement building, how to render some political action important. They also understood – in varied and sometimes oppositional ways – how crucial it is to organise in women-only radical action.

These are important actions and lessons that remain with us. Even when we do not fully grasp how profound that moment's symbolism is, it is no accident that at a time when so much of historic South African women's radical activist work has been erased, denied, obfuscated, maligned and pushed out of public memory, this march will not be erased. Even in the tamest representation of how it was possible to organise tens of thousands of women to the Union Buildings, it stands as "ferocious affirmation" well into the future.

Finally, Jordan's poem importantly reminds her reader/listener of those who would not join these women, and asks questions about who will join and stand apart from the future these women created. She reminds us that women's action is easy to celebrate retrospectively for those who have no real interest in creating a world friendly to women, a world fully owned by all.

This final line *"we are the ones we have been waiting for"* reminds us that women have to change the world through audacious action, and that we have it in us. It is a line that has been echoed across the works and movements of various African and African-world political movements since then. The award-winning African American women's musical sensation *Sweet Honey in the Rock* turned the phrase into a song, Alice Walker turned it into a book title, the radical Blackwomen who founded Blackwash turned it into a slogan for a new movement, even if that same phrase was later sometimes used patriarchally against them. That poem was inspired by the women who marched on the Union Buildings on 9 August 1956; Jordan names it a commemoration of these women's political work. It is a hopeful poem, and one that serves now as a reminder not just of June Jordan's genius, but also to us as women living in South Africa today of the women we come from, live in the midst of, and offers an important vision of ourselves and who we can be. As a South African woman and feminist, I have no doubt that we are up against some more tough times. The backlash continues to mutate more virulently than ever and we need to keep up with the business of crafting and recrafting new feminist strategies and tools. We cannot ever rest on our laurels. The high levels of violence against women, queers and gender non-conforming people, all of which are categories that leak into each other, are real; the intimate femicide, rape, routine sexual harassment are clear evidence. The increasingly brazen, spectacular violent masculinities in public political and popular culture remind us constantly how far away we are from a country in which gender is not used as a weapon to terrorise and annihilate.

While we have clear ideas of the work women in different groupings did in order to make the historic march possible, we are often at a loss as to what a new women's movement might look like. Many are pointing to this frustration when they repeatedly declare that the women's movement in South Africa is dead. They have a very set idea of what such a movement should do – take to the streets in the kinds of numbers that trade unions can marshal and shut down cities for a day, organise in the manner of the Women's March.

I am ambivalent about South African Women's Month because I wish there was less to complain and worry about, less to work against as far as the state of gender in the nation. I wish that one August we would actually be able to have a real celebration of how far we have come. I look forward to the August when we will not have to contend with doublespeak from those in elected positions of power, when the legal justice system will not be a huge violent patriarchal matrix, when violent masculinities will no longer hold us hostage, when little girls, boys and children of all genders will not be bludgeoned into submission to the regimes of heteropatriarchy.

Discussing the phenomenon of August in post-apartheid South Africa with a few feminist friends and sisters again each year, we spend some time on the usual irritations. Each August, there is a high demand for speakers on women specifically and gender more broadly in order to be in line with what matters; feminists and gender activists are suddenly A-listers since everybody gets invitations to more events that s/he/they can get to; commissions to write, speak, workshop and sit on committees abound; and phones ring non-stop in an attempt to rent-a-feminist for every institution's themed programme.

However, annually, even as we laugh at the farce of it all and the paradox of how important this month and marking is, we pause after we have made all the jokes about rounding up all the country's feminists and disappearing, going into hiding for the month. It is wonderful that the 1956 March demands and retains memory even in a very patriarchal nationalist narrative, marked by a day and an entire month. I love knowing that more often than not smart women are featured as experts on a range of topics on more radio and television shows than not, that intelligent women are everywhere, whether I agree with them or not. It makes me hopeful for what a truly free future looks like. It brings me joy to remember that Prof Fatima Meer, activist, feminist, intellectual was born in this month even if she has since transitioned to the ancestral realm.

It also brings me joy to remember that in August 2012 it was a celebratory march led by the African National Congress Women's League (ANCWL) that was disrupted by members of the 1in9 Campaign declaring "no cause for celebration". This moment of confrontation between different generations of women activists was an important reminder that the battle is not won. When so many women live in perpetual fear, and have little recourse in state institutions against that fear, we do need to temper our celebration. And the seasoned activists of the ANCWL recognised the importance of marking the moment of silence demanded by the younger feminists in purple shirts. Even if this acquiescence was tacit acknowledgement of their own duplicity with the strengthening of an increasingly patriarchally violent ruling party and government.

In 2016, however, the self-induced women's month love-fest was punctured by an inconvenient reminder that could not be brushed aside. On 6 August, at the Independent Electoral Commission's ceremony to announce results and declare the elections free, fair and peaceful, four women stood up and insisted that we reflect on how democracy fails women. Clad in black, they stood in front of the presidential podium, holding up placards, one of which implored us to #RememberKhwezi. Simamkele Dlakavu, Tinyiko Shikwambane, Naledi Chirwa and Amanda Mavuso reminded us that it had been ten years since the Jacob Zuma rape trial that introduced the word and garment "khanga" into everyday South African parlance.

When Pregs Govender posted on her Facebook page the four women's placards against a background of the four leaders of the 1956 march, what she communicated visually was unambiguous. Pregs Govender's own record as a unionist, anti-apartheid feminist activist, and as the only member of parliament to have voted against her party, against the nuclear deal, marks her as a Blackwoman who does not bow down to party discipline at all cost. As this edited image travelled – Shikwambane in front of Moosa holding two placards with "I am 1 in 3" and "#", Mavuso in front of Ngoyi holding up "10 yrs later", Chirwa's hands held up "Khanga", and Dlakavu's sign was "Remember Khwezi" as she stood in front of the only surviving leader of the 1956 March, Sophia Williams-de Bruyn. The black and white background of the leaders of the 1956 march, holding pages with petitions signed by tens of thousands of women, introduced a specific reading of the 2016 women's protest.

Whereas the Women's March is on the official annual calendar, it is associated with the ruling party in the post-apartheid public. This is why it is so easy to associate women's collective organising as belonging legitimately to the ANCWL before all other women's formations. The four leaders of the historic march enter the narrative as a reminder that women's activism sits uncomfortably with heroic nationalism. The giant image of the 1956 leaders stood as legitimation, offering a reading of #RememberKhwezi protestors as located in a long tradition of women's radical organising in their own name.

In the minutes, days and weeks that followed, the question of legitimacy was everywhere in discussions of the #RememberKhwezi protest. The successful link with the 1956 leaders had to be expanded by some and contested by others. Some activists who see themselves as the legitimate heiresses of the 1956 tradition of women's radical organising exploded in rage against the 2016 protesters. "These young women are cheapening rape and the experience of survivors of violence," they claimed. It did not matter that some of them had publicly come out as rape survivors themselves. They were accused of illegitimate and disrespectful action, of simultaneous political opportunism and political immaturity and being the pawns of the politically powerful men who lead the Economic Freedom Fighters political party. It was inconceivable that women could act in their own name, even to some of the most powerful governing women who saw the protest as disrespecting the President.

Yet, in Govender's visual sign, the image of the 1956 women's march leaders stood as giants authorising the protest by the 2016 women protesters. In the photographic background were thousands more women. They replaced Jacob Zuma in the image, deflecting his centrality, and inviting a reading of Shikwambane, Mavuso, Chirwa and Dlakavu, as the heiresses and actors in a long line of women's radical action. Soon, Fezeka Kuzwayo, the woman named Khwezi in 2006 by the 1in9 Campaign, a feminist formation established to support her in her court case against Jacob Zuma, was again on everyone's lips. April 2016 marked ten years since the awful spectacle of her brutalisation because she had laid a charge of rape against the man who would be the president in 2016. In April 2006, Jacob Zuma was acquitted of raping Fezekile Kuzwayo at the end of a trial that authorised misogynist brutality on a scale that should have been impossible in a democratic South Africa.

In television interviews the day after, Kwezilomso Mbandazayo and Mpumi Mathabela, feminist leaders from the 1in9 Campaign, expressed their unqualified support of the 2016 protest, and informed the public that Khwezi had received their protest as recognition and as support from fellow feminists. A week later, in an evening radio interview, the only surviving member of the four from the 1956 Women's March, Sophia Williams-de Bruyn, spoke of the necessary courage of the four protesters, the validity of their concern and stated that she saw no contradiction between her action in 1956 and theirs in 2016.

It is true that the protesters are EFF members but this does not reduce them to EFF opportunists. Rather than the positions of Jacob Zuma and EFF leader Julius Malema, we should pay attention to what these feminists' actions said.

First, the four activists walked to the front in black while their party in red left the Results Operations Centre. They could have asked their comrades to join them, or acted in concert with them. It means something that they chose not to. What bodies adorn and perform in political action matters. Rather, they chose to walk up, dressed in black, a colour that would not immediately associate them with any particular party. It must have been obvious to them that being dressed in their organisation's red would immediately work against them. It would reduce their important political action to the business of legitimacy and masculine power. To those hostile to the Economic Freedom Fighters, these women would be read as disruptive, undisciplined and badly behaved. The disapproval would trump any validity their message might have. After all, these same adjectives are used against the increasingly effective strategies used by EFF parliamentarians to delegitimise the governing party's majority in the legislature.

Second, Dlakavu, Shikwambane, Mavuso and Chirwa chose a key moment in the performance of democracy to remind us of what else this year marks. It was the South African public they were in conversation with. They chose to neither interrupt nor threaten President Zuma. Indeed, he was unaware of what was unfolding until the commotion alerted him. He was not the addressee. What they disrupted was the hypocrisy at the heart of the rainbow nation.

Importantly, as their action suggests, the hypocrisy was that of the electorate and voting public. Another round of free and fair elections are hailed as cause for celebrating the successes of the new dispensation. They are part of the pomp and ceremony of freedom and a country that works democratically. However, for these women the farce of democracy relies on the unacknowledged or trivialised scourge of gender-based violence. Shikwambane's "I am 1 in 3" is a stark reminder of the ever-presence of sexual assault, written in red like the blood the silenced/airbrushed victims and survivors bleed. They were reminding those in that hall as well as millions more watching in live broadcasts of the underbelly of this celebration. Nationalism is violent. There may be successful elections but women are still unfree and when Khwezi – Fezekile Kuzwayo, who also went by Fezeka – stood up, she was battered and exiled. Having pushed her out of view – and most South Africans were unaware that she had long returned – what Wambui Mwangi has elsewhere called "misogynist male interpreters and patriarchal narratives" tidied her out. These women, unlike many of their peers who sat with their political parties and celebrated the violence of narrative and the successes of an election, refused to be complicit with the erasure of women's daily realities in a democratic South Africa. "10 yrs later", Mavuso's sign reminded us, the patriarchal nationalists had returned to business as usual. Like the 1in9 banners, they insisted that there was no cause for celebration.

And while their EFF membership made them prime targets for accusations of hypocrisy given Malema's own 2006 rape apologist comments against Khwezi, seeing these women as only EFF pawns requires that we not take them seriously, that we airbrush everything in their lives except that which we can use against them. Malema was not part of their protest. They made this decision. To re-insert him as a way to dismiss them is violence. It requires that we embrace the very hypocrisy they challenge. Feminists located in other political parties like the Democratic Alliance, the African National Congress or the United Democratic Movement do not have to apologise as long as they toe the party line and can accept as supreme law the discipline of the organisational hierarchy.

Chirwa's sign read "Khanga", gesturing ambiguously. On the one hand, a khanga is an item of clothing African women wear daily and unspectacularly in many parts of the continent, that has sociality, aesthetic cultures and a politics much written about in East Africa. This item was used to belittle Khwezi/Fezeka as undressed during the court case. That demands repetition. Fezeka dressed herself like many East and Southern African women do and had this used against her. On the other, "I am Khanga" was the poem Kuzwayo wrote, published in 2008. In it, she writes:

> I wrap myself around the curvaceous bodies of women all over Africa
>
> I am the perfect nightdress on those hot African nights
>
> The ideal attire for household chores
>
> I secure babies happily on their mother's backs

Am the perfect gift for new bride and new mother alike

Armed with proverbs, I am vehicle for communication between women

I exist for the comfort and convenience of a woman

But no no no make no mistake …

I am not here to please a man

And I certainly am not a seductress

Please don't use me as an excuse to rape

Don't hide behind me when you choose to abuse

You see

That's what he said, my Malume

The man who called himself daddy's best friend

Shared a cell with him on Island for ten whole years

He said I wanted it

That my khanga said it

That with it I lured him to my bed

That with it I want you is what it said

But what about the NO I uttered with my mouth

Not once but twice

And the please no I said with my body

What about the tear that ran down my face as I lay stiff with shock

In what sick world is that sex

In what sick world is that consent

In the same world where the rapist becomes the victim

The same world where I become the bitch that must burn

The same world where I am forced into exile because I spoke out?

This is NOT my world

I reject that world

My world is a world where fathers protect and don't rape

My world is a world where a woman can speak out

Without fear for her safety

My world is a world where no one, but no one is above the law

My world is a world where sex is pleasurable not painful

"Khanga" on a placard implored the witnessing public to remember that women's bodies belong to themselves in a just world. The poem – Fezeka's own words – was in that room that night, hauntingly reminding us that "This is NOT my world/I reject that world". The world rejected in the poem is a patriarchally violent one in which men have legitimacy and nothing women do for themselves and in their own name matters. Ironically, in the responses by the leading women of the governing party, centring two patriarchal men – Zuma and Malema – is re-creating that world, even as the four women in front of them tried to unmake it, reminding us of the urgency of crafting the kind of world that can belong to women.

Many of us located in religious, educational, corporate or political institutions do not merely function as pawns of the patriarchal men in leadership and management. Their association does not inform every living breathing experience of women. This too is a reminder contained in the poem, and echoed in the #RememberKhwezi protest. Therefore, understanding these women as pawns requires the deliberate phallic re-insertion of men who are not in the frame of reference and minimising what the women's choices and bodies communicate. It also undermines the complicated layered lives that human beings live.

The #RememberKhwezi protesters are EFF members. They are also much more that offers no contradiction to their chosen protest action in August 2016. Two of the protesters were at the Results Operations Centre with press passes. One of them publishes regular opinion pieces in print media and has an occasional column for a major weekly newspaper. Reading her columns and public essays leaves no doubt about her ongoing commitment to Black women's activist traditions, narratives and uplift. Her community work in education and firing up the imagination of children in marginal communities predates the existence of the EFF. Returning constantly to questioning power in ways that are innovative and incisive, Dlakavu's decision to form part of #RememberKhwezi makes perfect sense.

A second hosts her own radio show on a university campus, and has previously co-hosted a women's talk show on national television with three women, two of whom are prominent feminist media powerhouses. Again, here is a woman whose radio show constantly probes the intersections of legal institutions and transforming societal power. Shikwambane's legal degree intersects with her media experience to probe especially the ways in which women's lives can matter differently.

One of the #RememberKhwezi protesters was a founder

member of #TransformWits; she has worked closely with different parts of the student movement, including #RhodesMustFall and the #RUReferenceList.

Mavuso's and Chirwa's positions as student leaders on university campuses often requires that they be the unpopular voice negotiating urgent political concerns and getting stereotyped as frightening man-haters. For Mavuso, feminist politics and self-identification are constantly in need of defence, even (and especially) within party culture.

All four protesting women were key members of #FeesMustFall and #EndOutsourcing. All four of them were either senior or postgraduate students at a leading South African university at the time of the protest. One of them is a member of the 1in9 Campaign, the organisation founded to support Khwezi in her 2006 court case.

The complexity that makes up the substance of women's lives is all inconvenient when we do not want to listen to the anger, experiences and voices of women. In Johannesburg, there had been a 1in9 public event to mark ten years since the end of the rape trial a few weeks before the #RememberKhwezi event exploded onto national news. There had been minimal media coverage of the event. The 1in9 march to commemorate the day of Fezeka's rape in November 2016, a few weeks after her death, was met with equal silence.

There was minimal media coverage of the University of Fort Hare students who marched down Oxford Street on 9 August 2016 carrying placards that shouted "My body is not an object to be analysed nor owned" and "You may look away but you can never again say you did not know". They, too, had chosen a strategic day to challenge South African gender power. But the media had turned away, in the main.

These are just a handful of examples of women organising and engaged in protest action across the country. Their visibility or invisibility is a function of where we sit, our reliance on media pathways and our investment in an increasingly untenable notion of what feminist movement looks like.

Reducing women to mere pawns is looking away. Pretending women cannot choose political actions is looking away and refusing to listen. However, the Fort Hare students, like 1in9 members who insist that there is "no cause for celebration", like #RUReferenceList and #RapeAtAzania and the #RememberKhwezi protestors echo the placard that says we cannot feign ignorance.

Dlakavu, Shikwambane, Mavuso and Chirwa are part of a groundswell of unapologetic feminist activism across our country, most of whom are not even EFF members. In concert, they are changing the face of what a feminist or women's movement looks like. They are impatient and they are tired. They speak in their own names and in defence of women.

Finally, this was a very important moment, one that demands that we all listen differently. These actions, whether in the public glare, or subjected to averted gaze, invite us to think about gender in relation to nationalism and to confront questions about what is wrong with separating them rhetorically. We need to constantly puncture the farce of the patriarchal narrative's lies that women are free in South Africa.

The #RememberKhwezi protest, like less visible protests in similar vein, was not about simply transgressing the boundaries of respectability, and/or embarrassing Zuma so much as exposing the generalised hypocrisy necessary for the performance of a patriarchally violent nation. Another clear example of this hypocrisy lies in the wide celebration of women's leadership and visibility in the new students' movement while ignoring the messy parts of the activism espoused by student activists. In other words, while there was obsessive attention paid to how many women's bodies could be seen in #FeesMustFall, as well as screening footage of student leaders like Nompendulo Mkhatshwa and Shaeera Kalla on a loop, with very few exceptions, the texture of the issues activists faced was less important than the content and complications that came with radical political action. In other words, while soundbites from Kalla's fiery speeches and Nompendulo's headwrapped defiant body were circulated as evidence of women taking charge and ushering in a new order, the constant harassment of Mkhatshwa and thirteen bullets in Kalla's back were too complicated a narrative and therefore needed airbrushing out.

The hypervisibility of radical student action on the one hand, and the refusal to engage with the brutality with which the state and public institutions dealt with them on the other hand was the reality for Fallists of all genders. What differed for women is the manner in which they were both held up as visually iconic as individuals and not engaged substantially. This ambivalence to women activists and women's activism is an older trope in South Africa's political sphere. This doublespeak is part of the hypocrisy the #RememberKhwezi protesters brought home. Doublespeak on gender talk rests on the refusal to engage the substance of women's radical political action by averting the gaze in search of a women's movement or re-centring men in avoidance of conversations that question the violence of heroic nationalism.

Having said that, the fact that so many hanker after a women's movement that looks a certain way, and therefore often have to confront the repeated question of whether a woman's movement is dead in South Africa is important. It reminds us, as Shireen Hassim's work has insisted for three decades, that we need an autonomous women's movement. Hassim's work constantly shows that the work of building and recognising this movement is not easy work. It is neither recuperative nor repetitive, but requires risk and new generative epistemes in order to make sense of what is unfolding in front of us. This recurring question reveals ongoing anxieties about the state of gender in our nation, and reveals more than a mere desire for a resolution.

It is only possible to answer yes to this question if we anticipate the large numbers of women taking to the streets I mentioned earlier, as well as the visible formation of mass-based organisations. This is a reasonable expectation, since claiming public space is a strategy much loved by all movements of the left, whether we have in mind the stripping in naked protest historically by Kenyan women's movements that has become so beloved of Fallist feminists in South Africa, the women's marches that culminated in the 1956 March to the Union Buildings, or reclaim the night and anti-patriarchal marches across the world.

While women's marches seldom attract the numbers that they once seemed to, and there are no attempts to come up with something akin to a Women's National Coalition, this decrying of a dying or dead women's movement is selectively attentive to history. When it is made, people forget why the Women's National Coalition worked, and how hard it was to ensure that it achieved its successes, choosing to focus in their nostalgia on the power of women from different political homes working together. They also eliminate the existence of formations like the Natal Organisation of Women and other similar province-based women's formations, or the specific processes that saw them weakened. Return is not simply possible. Nor has a singular approach ever advanced radical struggle.

There are many reasons why we do not see tens of thousands of women taking to the streets on a regular basis. Organising women in this way and to do so regularly continues to be a challenge in a context where the efficacy of such marches is under scrutiny. And in a context where women's public action simply receives muted or no coverage, we are asking the wrong questions if we expect such activism to find us in the comfort of our living rooms.

Feminist poet Audre Lorde is often quoted as warning against the use of the master's tool to topple hegemony. Marching against the state, where many seasoned women activists themselves are located, using tools that those in power now have intimate knowledge of can be as ironic as it is ineffective. This is part of the disillusionment with old forms and strategies associated with the anti-apartheid struggle. Feminist organisations like the 1in9 Campaign have long pointed this out. Fallist student activists understand the need for different kinds of formations, intimately working across old student organisations rather than within them.

Many of the older forms of women's movement organising were premised on a very clear relationship to the state, whether as enemy or potential partner. Such orientation no longer works in the current dispensation. This is not to say that there are no women's organisations that see the state as the enemy – indeed the more vocal ones occupy this position – given the free reign of violent masculinities in the political organisation of the nation as well as the ongoing brutalisation of sexual violence survivors within the legal justice system.

At the same time, many in the women's movement are part of the state, or invest in models of patient collaboration with the state. They are linked to this taming of subversive political language in which the successes of the current democracy have also been premised on directly weakening an autonomous women's movement. They have led to a more fractured women's movement than we have ever seen before. But they have also led to more vantage points from feminists than ever before. There have been significant gains in women's power and location since 1994, so we pretend to be perpetual outsiders at our own peril.

While there are various organisations and formations of women who organise for varied ends, they often do so separately, and unless you know or work with them, some of this action receives no media coverage. When they work outside of alliances and coalitions they are rendered invisible.

There is no question that the Rural Women's Movement and 1in9 Campaign, for example, do important work. Yet, many discussions of the South African women's movement often become obsessive reflections on the ANC Women's League – or expectations from women within the larger ruling party's ranks. While this may be well-intentioned, it also renders other spaces within the women's movement less visible.

It also reveals a hankering after a certain historic model of women's organising that has worked well to get the legislative framework we boast. However, it is clearer with each turn that those tools can get us no further than we are. The #RememberKhwezi protest is evidence of the urgency of new directions to re-energise women's movement. All four of those women are constantly engaged in feminist work, yet that moment generated more public contestation than the hard work they do in different organisations and institutions daily, and at great cost.

There is no question that feminist activism needs to be re-energised, and that we need to constantly evaluate the ways in which our strategies make it possible for us to be out of the frame. #RememberKhwezi is in the spirit of the many marches by the 1in9 Campaign and student feminist action like #RUReferenceList, Silent Protest, #RapeAtAzania and many other forms of action feminists organise regularly across the country. However, the reason it remains in the public imagination is due to these four feminists' savvy in how to protest in ways the nation could not avert its eyes from. It was a significant leap of the imagination, including questioning many of the tools that are as dear to activists in the women's movement as they are to other members of the left in South Africa.

The challenges are different. The enemy is more elusive if we need to think of what we fight as that which resides in a discernible enemy. However, there is no dearth of feminist activism, women's activism, in contemporary South Africa. It is simply that many are asking the wrong questions, looking for the wrong form – a form of feminist activism that will not help us shape the kind of society we need to create.

CHAPTER 4

Meeting Alice Walker

Along with millions of readers across the world, I have spent a significant amount of my reading life poring over Alice Walker's words in the last two decades. Although I was to fall in love with many other Black women writers in that time, hers was the first book by a Blackwoman I had ever read. The discovery in her work that I still return to has been echoed as much in the thousands of university students I have taught as it has in conversations with writers. It changes you to see yourself reflected for the first time in what you read. There were no plays, novels, short stories or poems by Blackwomen in my literary syllabus until my Honours year.

By the time I encountered Walker for the first time, almost by accident, I had been taught written literature in isiXhosa, isiZulu, English and Afrikaans. I had read individual essays by Blackwomen, usually in magazines. I remember an article in a woman's magazine, *Femina*, I think it was, that meant so much to me I must have read it a hundred times. I could not photocopy it, nor could I tear the page out; and, since the borrowed copy was a magazine no longer on the shelves, I could not buy it. It was an article by Lizeka Mda whose impact I will never forget.

So, my hunger for words by a Blackwoman on the page was real. I had known that I was meant to have a writing life since I was eight years old, and perhaps I needed an adult version of myself to affirm that dream. I loved the magazine *Tribute* and bought every issue I could after I left home, starting with Maud Motanyane's column, even when she moved to France for a year and wrote from there in ways I may have been too young to fully appreciate. Then I would read the rest of the magazine – cover to cover until well into my adulthood, through its various changes, until it folded. But until Walker, I had never held an entire book by a Blackwoman in my hand.

And so, even as an avid reader since primary school, I encountered Alice Walker outside the curriculum. I was registered in two literature departments at a leading university, and given what I now know about the volumes of Black women's writing, I can only shake my head. My own joy at discovering Walker as an undergraduate and my unapologetic admiration for her courage were part of the baggage I walked in with as she granted me an interview in September 2010.

Alice Walker was in South Africa as a guest of the Steve Biko Foundation, making her the second woman, after Mamphela Ramphele, to deliver the annual Biko lecture at my alma mater, the University of Cape Town, on Friday 9 September 2010.

As we wait for her – because I am so nervously excited I walk across Bertha Street from the University of the Witwatersrand campus on which I teach, to the Steve Biko Foundation offices in Braamfontein Centre twenty minutes earlier than I need to – the woman sent to photograph Alice Walker irritates me by questioning why there is so much fuss about her. She reveals herself unfavourably when it becomes clear that she is unaware of who Alice Walker is. I wonder out loud why this is who was allocated this brief by the paper.

But soon, Alice Walker arrives, while I have stepped out for another comfort break. When I walk back into the room, she is sitting behind a table next to her partner, with Nkosinathi Biko from the Steve Biko Foundation, whom I know from our UCT days, and the wonderful Obenewa Amponsah who ensured I was granted this interview. I walk straight to Alice Walker, breathless, and extend my hand in introduction.

"My name is Pumla Dineo Gqola, a womanist and a professor of literature", and hope I do not sound too rehearsed. She understands what I am saying with my words, with my spirit and with my body.

She is physically smaller in person than I had imagined, sports a short afro and a purple shawl hugs her hip. In my head, she is larger than life, and I talk to her constantly.

In response to my question about what this trip means to her, she speaks about her layered connection to South Africa. She had been active in anti-apartheid politics as part of her lifelong activism against racist violence and any form of injustice. But she also feels deep love and comradeship with both Winnie and Nelson Mandela. "I've always wanted to visit South Africa and have been arrested for it before. In fact, it was my pleasure and honour to be arrested with Maya Angelou."

Walker spoke of having been there with Winnie when she was banished to Brandfort, with her children, a place thought to be the middle of nowhere. "Many of us in the US suffered with her. I grew up in Georgia and so have a deep understanding of what it takes to be a soldier."

Later on the same day, speaking at 'An evening with Alice Walker', she elaborates on this connection, declaring "it is unusual for me to speak at a place where one of my most important teachers is also admired: Fidel Castro". The crowd roars and claps its approval. There is mutual recognition between Walker and the people who came to hear her read when she mentions Myanmar activist and author, Aung San Suu Kyi, who at the time is in her fifteenth year under house arrest, the brave Venezuelan president Hugo Chavez and Bolivian socialist president Evo Morales. The latter two are mentioned as part of a global shift away from the politics of imperialist mineral and land grab. The former affirms the importance of love for humanity in radical politics, like Biko's own legacy.

Walker is no stranger to criticism. The mixed responses to her third and best known novel, *The Color Purple*, for which she won the Pulitzer Prize for Fiction, partly illustrate this. In the United States, she was severely lambasted for shining a light on the misogyny that also exists in Black families, accused of judging Blackmen unfairly, and later for allowing a white director to be at the helm of the film adaptation of the same novel. It was inconvenient for many of these critics to pay attention to the manner in which the novel is really about the possibility of human transformation from violence to chosen gentleness, as well as from subjection to a life well lived. Interestingly, she would also later receive criticism for precisely this portrayal of the possibility of unlearning misogyny by some feminists. This novel, then, was criticised for being too hard on Blackmen, by anti-feminist Blackmen, and as too gentle on Mr_____, the novel's patriarch. Quite contrary to the allegation that her anti-racism could be placed in competition with her feminism, womanism allows for a vision of anti-racist feminism that places the lives of Blackwomen at the centre.

A woman who does not want to apologise for valuing herself is a dangerous thing.

In South Africa, many feminists continue to write about womanism as being a conservative form of gender consciousness. I have never been able to understand this, based on the writings of Walker, who obviously speaks a radical feminism. Walker published a definition of the word she coined in the same year as African feminist literary critic and cultural theorist, Chikwenye Okonjo Ogunyemi. Both definitions are unapologetic about womanism being feminist, and stress its valuation of Blackwomen and feminist imagination. The coincidence of two feminist women of the African world naming a specific feminism similarly without conversing is a delicious illustration of how we are all connected. It troubles those who need a more "factual" account that flattens how living beings fit into the world. Neither Walker nor Ogunyemi conceives of womanism as anything but a radical feminism of colour. Walker writes "womanist is to feminist as purple to lavender" in *In search of our Mothers' Gardens*. Womanism is also coined by both with Black women's literary and other creative cultures in mind.

The novel she refers to most often to illustrate points in interviews, including in hers with me, *Possessing the Secret of Joy*, was to earn her a different round of criticism, this time from some African feminists. This group took exception to her criticism of female genital mutilation and her right to speak about this as an outsider. Her response to this criticism has illustrated the many ways in which Walker refuses to exile herself from any human condition. As we discuss how she determines which form an idea is to take, I refer to her statement about how characters in novels "do not leave her alone" until she writes them. I use the phrase "bug you".

She disagrees with my word choice.

"They do not bug me. They are just present ... until I understand what has happened to them – wounded them." This is what happened with *Possessing the Secret of Joy*. But her poems and essays come to her in a form close to what she eventually shares with the world.

Her womanism is a resolute refusal to look away from such wounding, in as much as it is a commitment to recognising her loving connection to other living beings on the planet. This is not true of all Black feminisms, and need not be, and this is why it is sometimes important to show this difference. Because words are so powerful, they often frighten even the writer. Yet, Audre Lorde insisted that what is important needed to be said, even at the risk of misunderstanding and violence.

In that room with Walker, I want to know whether being so severely criticised for speaking her mind over twenty-six books and numerous interviews gets easier.

"I have a greater level of indifference. You start to understand that you're like any other creation, so if I say things that people take offense to, that's who I am. That's what you get from me."

She adds that we are all entitled to live and that criticism is not always important.

"Would you criticise a pecan tree? Really, what's the point? That's the place you get to."

I pause and laugh.

And I realise that she is saying something about letting go of the need for approval and external validation, which is so central to how women are raised all over the world. Given that she will speak her mind, "irregardless" (her word), she has learnt this indifference. Importantly, she also adds thoughts on how she understands why people who have been wounded can think "any criticism can be used against all of us".

I am glad to hear this from a writer whose unfashionable perspective on the world is likely to continue to earn her detractors. I tell her I look forward to this experience, as a writer who is sometimes afraid of her own voice. Her courage also continues to be rewarded by her readers' appreciation of her vision and generosity.

In the interview she speaks softly. She declares later that evening at the State Theatre in Tshwane that she is soft-spoken. This almost seems like a contradiction, save for the fact of her clear gentleness during the interview.

I end the interview with a very clear sense of having had a conversation with an incredible human being, not a star, but a generous, attentive person. I realise that the power in her written work is like this power I feel in the interview at the Steve Biko Foundation offices. It only lasts twenty-five minutes, but for that period, turned towards me, in conversation, it is as though we are the only people in the room.

I ask her to sign copies of her books. I only bring two, even though I have multiple versions of all her books. At the last minute, I am too shy to offer her the copy of my first book I had brought as a gift.

I do not know what I expected, and I would have been thrilled by the opportunity to meet her. But there she was with no entourage, no restrictions, no apologies for being on the planet in her own fashion. I realise that the Walker I encounter on that Tuesday morning is very much the Walker who speaks to an adoring audience, and dances to Simphiwe Dana and Sibongile Khumalo's genius later that night at the State Theatre. She is the Walker many of us encounter in her work, the Walker we return to time and again. This is the Walker who galvanises and inspires me to live courageously, who is my compass, and the writer who has written a book for every season in my life. In my late twenties, I once spent a heartbroken weekend in bed in my sixteenth-floor flat with the sun shining in, crying, drinking tea and reading *The Way Forward is with a Broken Heart*. Sometimes the conversation I have with her is that literal. It is her courage and her joyful embrace of life that makes it possible for her to change and save our lives so many times. It is this Walker that helps us believe that "we are the ones we have been waiting for", the line from a June Jordan poem that she made the title of one of her books.

I ask my final question, given to me the previous weekend by Madi, whose spirit I chose to love in the same year I discovered Walker, "What have you learnt from your best friends – no matter what form they come in?" That life and this planet is wonderful, "so even if I am weeping as I am writing, there is joy because I know where I came from, from sharecroppers. And how my mother never asked me to come and wash dishes if I was reading. So, to be able to take all that nurturing and that thoughtfulness and to go and to learn how to do this. Every tear comes with laughter."

"I cannot get over the wonder of this world. I live in a state of wonder … it is all connected", and living life in both contemplation and wonder is rewarding.

"It is not for nothing that my name is Alice," she quips.

CHAPTER 5

Living like a girl

We have all always known girls who did not act or think the way they were supposed to, even as children. I do not just mean the badly behaved outcasts. I mean those who were not quite convinced by ideas of what girls should be.

I was one those girls. My little-girl self enjoyed many things that supposedly did not go together. I loved climbing trees, crawling into cupboards, and scurrying up anything that had a foothold and somewhere to place my hand. My passion for using my body to explore my surroundings did not temper my interest in more conventional girl interests. I loved playing with dolls, playing on the swing, baking mud cakes with my sisters and drinking delicious imaginary liquids from our tea sets. In role-play I would imitate my mother and father equally, depending on the mood I was in. My favourite superhero was Hulk. It still is, although I developed my appetite for girl superheroes quite early on, hoping one day to discover one that looked like me.

While our parents allowed my sisters, brother and me to explore what we liked, when my grandmother visited I knew that the positions I found most comfortable were inappropriate. Gently at first, but later with some degree of irritation, Nkgono would instruct me to sit with my legs closed *all the time*. I have always preferred to sit with my legs close to my body, or with my legs parted or in a variety of poses that feel comfortable. Sitting like a girl still feels restrictive, although these are the positions I assume in public spaces now. Alone, or in my own or the homes of my friends, I continue to sit with my legs close to my upper body. I learnt the lessons my grandmother imparted. Where I felt comfort, Nkgono saw danger in various guises.

Perhaps she was thinking of how this unfettered comfort in my own body would make me vulnerable to sexual exploitation. Many women are taught to try to carry our bodies in specific ways in order to be safer to sexual violence. Or maybe, the danger she saw was that I would eventually turn into an adult who was not a woman in appropriate feminine, respectable ways to marry. She must have known from her own life how little room there would be for a girl who had the ridiculous notion that sitting was about comfort for girls. Nowadays, I choose to think that she was trying to cushion me from a string of vulnerabilities she suspected awaited me when I stepped out into the world.

From her lived experience, she understood that it was not a country and world hospitable to someone like me. Sebabatso Ramapepe was born between the world wars in Lesotho, in a colonised country called a British protectorate where girls' education was not guaranteed. She had moved to marry my grandfather, Sakiya Gugushe, and together they had moved to Johannesburg. As a woman who has several times packed up my life to move across the country or to countries on another continent, I know something about the angst and thrill of the unknown departure to start a new life. Still, my own movements happened after 1994, and I had middle-class safety nets in the form of multiple degrees, scholarships or employment. My Nkgono was barely an adult when she left Lesotho, the only country she had ever known, for another country to live with a man she hoped to build a happy life with. I am both awed and stunned by the courage and wilfulness it took to be this woman in the first half of the twentieth century. It is obvious that her life very directly made mine possible – not just in the biological sense, but in ensuring the kind of woman my mother could become, and as I grow older I am surprised by how much of Sebabatso is in the fabric of my view of the world.

Once she had settled in Crown Mines in Johannesburg, with her teacher-turned-clerk husband, and as she became a mother, I cannot imagine the terror of watching the dawn of apartheid with five small children, the vulnerabilities to white men's violence and Black men's sexism. Now I mull over the things I do not know about her as a young woman, what she was able to create in a context that sought to contain her. She can be forgiven for wanting to shield me from a racist, sexist world that did not care about what Blackgirls wanted, and one that violated them as a matter of course.

When I asked her why she insisted on correcting my sitting, her answers did not satisfy me. I do know that as she corrected me, she would tell me to sit like a girl. When I read the exquisite short stories of the pioneering South African feminist author, Miriam Tlali, in which she writes often about women characters travelling between Johannesburg, Bloemfontein and Lesotho, I often wonder about my grandmother's trips. Tlali's women characters constantly negotiate how to escape the snares of opportunistic, predatory white railway officials in inventive ways. They are wonderful examples of feminist imagination – unflinchingly attentive to how racism and patriarchy create specific areas of vulnerability for Blackwomen under apartheid. But her stories are also feminist in the kinds of strategies the writer puts at the disposal of her characters. Sometimes when I read Tlali, I wonder about my Nkgono, older, making and remaking that journey from one home to another.

As my grandmother continued to police my posture, I noticed that none of my boy cousins had to sit uncomfortably, because they were boys. Later, I understood too that a penchant for climbing was not deemed appropriate girl behaviour by others, although she was indifferent to this. I was a chubby, clumsy child who climbed passionately but inelegantly and therefore fell constantly. Nkgono must have realised that climbing would soon be impractical for a girl and later woman's life. Mama feared I would lose an eye, break a limb or crack my skull. After each fall, and sometimes before my tears dried, I would be challenging my little body to further heights. My body still bears some of the scars – on my inner eyelid, the side of my face, my knees and shins. I wear these barely visible nicks and scrapes with a joy even greater than the one I derive from my inked skin. My skin has long let go of traces of my numerous bruises and even these scars are hard to spot to the inattentive eye. But they are there. My body carries the memory of these scrapes, scars, bruises and tears like heaps of stories of joy and pain. Mine is a well-lived-in body that continues to be stretched to new adventures.

If being taught to sit like a girl had been my initial introduction to proper ways of being a girl, school drove this point home. In watching my primary school playmates, and being further socialised into being a good girl, there were constant echoes of Nkgono's words. My friend Pamela, whose name we all pronounced *Pah-meh-lah,* disliked dresses, dolls, tea sets and playing dress up. We all disliked needlework, and the annual sewing projects made little sense. It took a lifetime to finish those dresses we produced. They were too large for dolls and too small for any girls we knew, in strange brightly coloured fabrics none of us found pretty. Remembering to fold the material we took months to sew was a nuisance. Ensuring that we lost neither thread nor needles were our first lessons in anxiety. Most of Pam's friends were boys and she enjoyed their company and games. Yet, she was required to wear her shirt under a black tunic we called a "gym dress" for school uniform. She felt awkward in a dress but was punished when she arrived at school wearing grey trousers. Pam was denied permission to take gardenwork in place of needlework as a subject. More dramatically, she was often told to stop thinking she was a boy, to act like a girl, and fight her "tomboy" urges.

Watching her collectively bullied by children and some adults brought home the lessons of what happens to girls who do what they want. So, at school, many of us hid who we really were in order to act like proper girls. But we admired Pam, and our fascination grew. We also learnt that our full selves as girls were too much for school, and that we needed to keep those parts hidden, and to show support for transgressive girls in coded ways. A few of us remained her friends even if we never fully revealed the parts of ourselves that were drawn to her capacity to be so fully herself. And often we stood up for her when others sought to shame her back into her place as a girl, although this also depended heavily on how threatened we were by the shamers.

The older we grew, the more acutely I felt this sense of injustice – as I sprouted breasts and started bleeding every month, and as the differences between girls and boys became starker. I was taught that there were good boys and bad boys. Good boys could be friends. One of the good boys wrote me my first love letter, but he was also bad in the ways that made him interesting to have as a friend when you were a girl. He was friends with Pamela too.

But mostly, girls and boys were supposed to be very different. The older we grew, the more frequent the reminders, even though we were all still little children. As a parenting adult, I marvel at how small children are until the age of 12, especially when I realise how many ideas about gender we had been taught by then, and how sexual some of these were.

Girls had to wait for boys to approach them rather than initiating contact. Boys could have several girlfriends and be admired for such prowess. Girls had to keep their virginity in check otherwise they would have to leave school, even when they were impregnated by known sexual predators. Even when hurt, girls had to control themselves. And boys who stepped out of line and were not boy enough were equally open to ridicule, but they did not have to leave school.

Being a girl was a mess of emotions. I liked being a girl. But I hated how strangers sexualised me. A man in his twenties once asked me whether I had grown hair on different parts of my body yet, before I had finished primary school. This was a man who had previously treated me like a younger sister. I had the presence of mind to tell my mother what he had said and to point him out to her the next time we encountered him. Not one to hold back when a loved one is pained, my mother tore into him, but I continued to avoid him until he moved away many years later. His comment reminded me that I was not his sister, that he felt entitled to humiliate me, and that I could very quickly move from intimacy to danger. At the same time, I was aware of how many times girls were required to keep ourselves in check, so I understood that his treatment of me anchored in the fact that I was a girl.

It did not come from the place of love as my Nkgono's unwelcome lessons about my body did. As an adult woman, understanding this difference has helped me deal with the resentment, guilt and shame from these lessons. While both these lessons were communicating to me that I should be less comfortable in my body, I had no doubt that my Nkgono would protect me from danger with no hesitation. The correction was confusing to me, and I assumed she just disliked me, and proceeded to feel enormous shame for assuming this. The shame was two-fold: first, because I adore my mother, it felt disloyal to her to resent my grandmother; second, everybody is supposed to know their grandmother cherishes them. After all, my Nkgono has named me Dineo. How sinful is it to feel anything but loving gratitude for a woman who sees in you multiple treasures?

Nkgono was a woman who did not always do what she was supposed to do. Her life shows this. Pamela was a girl who did what she liked. This does not mean it came easily to them. Perhaps, they were the kinds of women for whom normal was too hard. Some of my friends agreed that normal could feel like a prison. Others thought that "normal" as defined for us was not so bad.

Although these forceful ways of being like a girl or boy never came automatically to me, I moved from instance to instance and in between negotiated how to be myself. It was therefore with nothing short of delight that, at fifteen, I discovered the word "feminist". I embraced it wholeheartedly. I loved finding out there were many other girls all over the world who agreed on the unfairness of what we first called sexism and later patriarchy, and were trying to end it. The friend I discovered it with described feminist as a girl who will not be a doormat, thinks girls can be anything they want and will defend other girls.

As my feminism grew, I understood that patriarchy is a global system that keeps people locked into roles that may not fit who they really feel themselves to be or want to be. It is a system that thrives on opposition and restriction, and one that has evolved over centuries and spread to cover almost all societies. Feminism is a global movement of people who know patriarchy is unjust, and that human beings are not primarily flawed and in need of training into rigid roles of girl and boy, man and woman. Feminism says there is no automatic relationship between the sex encoded in our chromosomes and the way we want to dress, speak, love or dream. This is why we have to be trained into these roles – sometimes through seduction but mostly through fear. Feminists reject patriarchy's insistence that human beings come in two, oppositional sexes: one soft, emotional and inferior, the other hard, rational and superior. Feminism also rejects the idea that desire only comes in one form, across genders. We believe that such behaviours and attitudes are learnt as we are raised, or socialised into them. Therefore, a different world is possible since patriarchal behaviour and attitudes can be unlearnt. Feminists have made a commitment to fighting, undermining and ultimately ending this system of patriarchy that is violent and oppressive to human beings, but is so romanticised and entrenched that some religions and cultures normalise it.

Whereas thinking about patriarchy as a global phenomenon could have crushed me had I really grasped it, the idea that there were millions of others like me who felt strongly that these gender scripts were limiting and forceful was a homecoming. I had found my tribe and knew it had a name that would allow me to identify its members more easily sometimes. It is still an enormous joy to me to be part of this earth-wide chosen community.

While there are many feminist strands, which is to say different kinds of feminism, there are also many core principles. The commitment to actively oppose and end patriarchy is one. The recognition that patriarchy works like other systems of oppression, like racism and capitalism, to value some people and brutalise others is another area of agreement. Like other systems of oppression, it also requires the support of many members of the groups it oppresses. Just like some victims of racism believe that white people are more advanced, better suited to leadership and are in other ways superior to Black people, so too many women believe men are natural leaders and women meant to obey.

This helped me understand that fighting conditioning is hard, and that even transgressive people sometimes propped up this system, that the world was not divided tidily between good and bad people. My Nkgono and Pam and I could defy appropriate behaviour for girls and women, and still find joy in other aspects deemed normal for people like us. It would be a contradiction sometimes. Contradictions make us human, although, beyond a certain point, they can also make us hypocrites.

The third aspect that drew me further into the fold of my new tribe was the realisation that feminists want human beings to have real choice over their lives, sexuality and bodies. Women should be able to decide what to do with their bodies freely and without punishment or threats of violence. Feminists believe a woman should be able to choose what to do with her body, that reproduction is a choice not a destiny, that women are entitled to sexual pleasure if they desire it without judgement, and to terminate pregnancies if they wish safely, and that nothing women do with their bodies is "asking" for violence.

All feminists believe that violence is the way in which patriarchy strengthens its hold on human society and keeps women afraid. I devote a chapter in my previous book, *Rape: a South African nightmare*, to how important this fear is, what I call the female fear factory. This violence keeps women unfree by forcing us to surrender choice by sitting, dressing and walking "like girls" in order to be safe. Patriarchy ensures that the threat of social censure, rape, battery, sexual harassment and poverty train women to police themselves and each other. If we believe that we cause rape, then we are less likely to feel free to move about where and when we like. If we fear being branded loose, ugly or fat, we will curb our appetites, transform our bodies in order to better make ourselves desirable in the market for marriage. Feminists see marriage as a particularly complicated institution, and one that patriarchy cannot survive without. But feminists also believe that all institutions can be changed. So, there are as many feminists who marry as there are who reject marriage as irredeemably patriarchal.

As I grew in my feminism, I realised that there were many other areas of agreement. However, feminists do not agree on everything. As feminists we take very different stances on pornography, prostitution, beauty, whether men should call themselves feminists and whether violence can ever be a strategy against patriarchy. I have changed my mind about which feminist arguments I find most convincing over the years on pornography, whether to call it prostitution or sex-work, and hyperfemininity.

Beauty is another contentious issue for feminists. All feminists recognise that there is a global patriarchal beauty industry that depends on women feeling either inadequate, on the one hand, or like they are too much, on the other. Therefore for feminists shaving, waxing, dieting and vaginal douching require women to believe their bodies need fixing and to commit to doing this work of making their bodies less threatening. Such bodies are recognisable as valuable and attractive, ready for consumption for men's desire. Most feminists nonetheless believe that not all work women do on their bodies is for the eyes of men, that women sometimes derive pleasure from practices that were initially created to keep women down.

While many women will readily admit that voting, access to education and professions, the right to own property and be paid equal salaries to men for equal work are all feminist battles their lives have been enriched by, feminism nonetheless scares them.

I understand that sexist media paints feminists as unnecessarily angry, frightening, killjoys. If patriarchy fears and demonises feminists, we are doing something right. Feminists are rogues – unapologetically disrespectful of patriarchal law and order, determined to create a world in which choice is a concrete reality for all.

In the company of these feminists, I love, laugh, cry, dance, watch as no one flinches at the variety of gender, sexual and other expressions. Normal is a Batman-suit-clad child on his pink bicycle, the adorable boy in a Spiderman suit and a pink handbag, and the little girl with lipgloss whose soccer skills suggest she is a future Portia Modise, a legend in the making.

Feminism has saved my life, allowed me to live in my skin lovingly, to speak in my own voice. I now know that girls who don't always do what they are supposed to are normal. Boys too. Another world is possible.

CHAPTER 6

When feminists fight

In August 2009, feminist painter, Bongi Bengu curated *Innovat1ve Women*, an exhibition comprising the works of ten Black women visual artists, including herself. The remaining nine ranged from emerging names to internationally acclaimed artists: Zanele Muholi, Ingrid Masondo, Lerato Shadi, Nandipha Mntambo, Nontobeko Ntombela, Senzeni Marasela, Usha Seejarim, Dineo Bopape and Ernestine White. Initially opening at Constitution Hill in Braamfontein, the show also travelled to the Bell-Roberts Gallery in Cape Town in September, and Kizo Gallery in Durban in November. The exhibition was partly funded by the national Department of Arts and Culture.

The exhibited artworks were provocative in the kinds of worlds they brought into collision, and their intertextuality left few established authorities untouched. This is because the artists chose playful registers to make sense of "the serious": they subverted the boundaries of the sacred and profane, and appropriated unfashionable visual and textual register in the design of Black feminist exchange. I wrote the catalogue essay for this exhibition and was struck as I viewed the artworks by how bold it was, and how very different the visual languages used by these Black women artists were. Part of my task for the catalogue essay was to read them separately and as a single curated project at the same time. As a feminist who is fascinated by the ways in which creative texts expand our senses of the world, and of our selves, I was reminded of the words of womanist theorist and literary scholar, Chikwenye Okonjo Ogunyemi, who has argued that African feminist literary trends place women at the centre of imagined universes in "thickly layered, revelatory scripts and distinct thrusts" producing "works that are physically energizing". Now, even as these words came to mind, I reminded myself that these were not literary texts; and I was cautious not to read the exhibition through a flattening lens. Literary scholars hold sacred two aspects of analytical praxis. First, we teach our students to always move from the meanings suggested by a text, rather than approaching literature with a preconceived wholly formed theory in need of application. Second, we remind them to never be so focused on content that they lose focus of the text's literariness, its form, structure and aesthetics as the very languaging of what it creates.

Now, although I have written and published on aspects of visual art and visual culture, I am trained as a literary critic and to a linked extent as a literary historian. Although there are specific orientations to criticism that are shared between the arts and differ from the social sciences, there are also specific ways of reading that have been developed within disciplines. Therefore, while an art historian, theatre or film scholar is trained to pay more attention to the form and language of creative sites and can therefore produce sophisticated literary criticism, I am aware of how informal and self-taught my visual reading praxis is. Yes, when I had a life partner who was an artist and art historian, I shamelessly and thirstily devoured as much of how he taught the discipline to his students as I did his reading lists. It also means that my friends who are art historians and art critics spend a lot of time explaining things to me about the evolution of visual registers. As a person with very few regrets, the one strong regret I do have is dropping Art History as a subject in my first year at the University of Cape

Town. I gave it three weeks and decided it was not for me. How strangely life works out. And, no, I am not one of those people who believe Cultural Studies gives us all the tools we need to make sense of cultural production. Call me old fashioned.

This is some of the baggage I brought to the *Innovat1ve Women* exhibition. Each artwork displayed was conceived and executed differently. At the same time, the exhibition space rehearsed a coming together of ideas about embodiment, reinscription, experimentation with voice and discovery.

The Constitution Hill exhibition was to be opened by the (then) Minister of Arts and Culture, Lulu Xingwana, who became the Minister of Women, Children and People Living with Disabilities, after President Jacob Zuma's parliamentary reshuffle in October 2010. Arriving more than an hour later than scheduled to officiate, Xingwana walked about the space with the artworks and then promptly departed without delivering her opening speech. In the Minister's sudden absence, a woman staff member from the Ministry explained that Xingwana had been urgently called to attend to an unnamed, urgent matter, and continued to read the Minister's prepared opening address.

The speech made generic mention of African women and art in patriarchal history, commented on patterns of historic neglect of women's creativity, listed some governmental commitments to transformation of South African society, and linked contemporary artistic production to centuries-long traditions of beading. The speech also glossed over the occasion of the exhibition in August, South African women's month. No mention was made of any of the artists whose art was on display, no references where made to their artwork. I remember thinking this was a speech that could have been presented at any exhibition of any type of artwork as long as the artists were African women.

Several months later, in early 2010, the South African media broke the story of how Minister Xingwana had left the Constitution Hill opening because she disapproved of some of the exhibited artworks. In what quickly became a media frenzy in which anonymous sources were cited, there emerged a picture of an embattled Ministry of Arts and Culture as it transitioned from Pallo Jordan's tenure to Xingwana's.

In one of her responses to the hullabaloo, Xingwana, speaking through her Departmental website, asserted:

> [c]ontrary to media reports, I was not even aware as to whether the 'bodies' in the images were of men or women or both for that matter. My reaction was guided by the view that these 'artworks' were not suitable for a family audience. I noticed that there were children as young as three-years-old in the room.

Like many of us who were unconvinced by such defence, poet and academic Gabeba Baderoon responded:

> Minister, I invite you to look at art that challenges you, like that of Nandipha Mntambo and Zanele Muholi. That looking is an active and complicated experience that includes all the discomfort, shock, unsettling of established notions, new ideas and feelings that you appear to have had at the Innovative Women exhibition, and that together can amount to illumination. That is what art does. The problem with walking out of an exhibition is that you miss the many meanings that the works evoke, both separately and together. You miss what they create and unsettle, and therefore the possibility of transformation.

These two citations show up aspects of the public debate that resulted in early 2010. The first, excerpted from Minister Xingwana's press statement posted on her department's website and distributed to various media outlets, highlights Xingwana's motivation for leaving the exhibition opening. This statement throws up various seeming contradictions. Setting aside the ascription of gender neatly to the body, Xingwana lists the context of the exhibition as inappropriate. Her comments question the suitability of some of Zanele Muholi's and Nandipha Mntambo's photographs. Xingwana argues that these artists had produced content unsuitable for "a family audience", questions whether such photographs can be seen as art at all, and indeed problematises the validity of the very bodies on display. The Minister's attention is exclusively directed at the offending photographs from two of the artists, which Xingwana further dismisses later in the statement as:

> not works of art but crude misrepresentations of women (both black and white) masquerading as artworks but rather than engaged in questioning or interrogating – which I believe is what art is about. Those particular works of art stereotyped black women.

Xingwana is further concerned about the possible safety and legality of the works on show when she later evokes her responsibility to protect children from pornography, in line with current South African legislation. It is interesting that Xingwana claims ignorance of the gender of the offending bodies since in both Mntambo's and Muholi's artworks, gender is made explicit in artist statements at the same time as calling gendered meanings into question. In other words, while gender obviously does not inhere in the body, both Mntambo and Muholi provide numerous clues to the gender of their subjects: in the artist statements where Muholi identifies her subjects here – as elsewhere – as Black lesbians, in Mntambo's own as the recognisable face and body in the offending photographs, and in other ways as will become clearer in my analysis of the artworks below. Given this simultaneous signification of the gender of the subjects as women, the framing of the exhibition as one by Black women artists concerned with how gender works, and Minister Xingwana's distaste as linked to the representations of the bodies she saw in the artworks, it is difficult to understand the contents of the statement above. Indeed, while there is much contestation among feminists globally on what constitutes pornography, there is relative consensus that its definition lies in the specific representations of nudity and/or nakedness, sexuality and bodies. Minister Xingwana's statement suggests both that she found the idiom of representation offensive as well as that she did not pay enough attention to the artworks to notice what they contained.

Minister Xingwana was correct in noting the presence of small children in that room, and some were considerably younger than three years old. I had brought my eighteen-month-old son with me, as I did to many other exhibitions. I would never expose him to pornography even if I had imagined he would be too young to understand. I doubt that the queer feminists and other parents who brought their small children would expose their children to age-inappropriate material either. However, unlike Xingwana, naked women's bodies do not automatically scream "pornography" to me, even as I remain an anti-pornography feminist. And I teach my children not to think of women's bodies as dirty, shameful, in need of covering, hiding or gratuitous display. These are important lessons for me as a feminist mother of a man and a boy, and as feminist aunt of nephews, given the many pressures they face to perform misogynist masculinities.

Infinitely more interesting to me in the Minister's responses cited above, however, are the many clues that she simply did not care to pay attention to what the exhibition suggested. As a seasoned activist who has fought for many gender-progressive policies and laws herself, Xingwana knows that context matters for how language creates meaning. She knows who and where things are said matters for powerplay. Had she paid attention, as Baderoon invites, she would have noted the consistent critique of stereotype and patriarchal tradition in the artworks on display. She would have been alerted to this by the artist statements, by the curatorial statement and by the artworks themselves.

In her open letter to Xingwana from which I excerpt, Gabeba Baderoon invites the Minister to revisit initial impression, embrace the discomfort that comes from artworks which do not show us what we are accustomed to or are comfortable with. Although I will return to the longer letter, this excerpt is useful because it illustrates both the agreement and the disagreement between Xingwana and Baderoon. Baderoon's outline of what art achieves: "illumination" and "transformation", as achieved through "discomfort, shock, unsettling of established notions, new ideas and feelings that [Xingwana] appear[s] to have had" rhymes with

Xingwana's claim that art should be "engaged in questioning or interrogating". Although Xingwana and Baderoon differ markedly on the relevance of this specific show and the analyses engendered by Muholi's and Mntambo's work, the two clearly agree on the general uses of art.

In what follows, I argue that this controversy illustrates something about the discourses on gender and public space in South Africa, with particular reference to Black women's embodiment, creativity and feminist imagination. The disagreement around the *Innovat1ve Women* exhibition offers an opportunity to surface what is energising and disruptive about Black feminist creativity in post-apartheid South Africa. This is read both in relation to responses from the state in the figure of one of its ministers, who also has a track record of anti-patriarchal activism, on the one hand, and the reactions of figures within the art critical world to both the exhibition and the Ministerial controversy.

What was missing for me in much of the controversy was an actual engagement with what the artworks said. This was as true – it is painful to admit – in most of the writing that jumped to defend Mntambo and Muholi specifically, as it was in Xingwana's public pronouncements. In other words, whereas the legitimacy of gender-progressive language and feminist imagination was at the heart of the contestation, the feminist artist and exhibition curator, Bengu was barely mentioned, and most of the artists who formed part of the exhibition were completely erased from the controversy. One would be forgiven for thinking that *Innovat1ve Women* was an exhibition solely by Nandipha Mntambo and Zanele Muholi.

My analysis illustrates the textures of competing articulations of gender-progressive representation that circulate in South Africa. The primary texts under analysis are select artworks from the *Innovat1ve Women* exhibition and Xingwana's press statements. I analyse the artworks in some detail, but even in this lengthy essay, there is much I want to say about the artworks that I omit, and I read Xingwana's response alongside other responses from Black feminists who weighed in on the furore.

setting the terms of the debate

Much of the response to the news coverage of the Minister's stance made connections between Xingwana's departure and her ignorance of how art works (for examples, see essays by Gail Smith, Eusebius McKaiser and Gender DynamiX's rebuttal), drew parallels between her dislike of Muholi's and Mntambo's work and apartheid censorship (examples include Gabeba Baderoon's open letter, Sean O'Toole's, Sally Evans' and Yvette Christiansë's public pieces) or insisted that Xingwana had acted in homophobic and anti-feminist ways (argued variously by Baderoon, Smith, McKaiser, Oppelt and myself). Organisations within the LGBTI community such as Gender DynamiX, the Forum for the Empowerment of Women (FEW), the Black lesbian NGO Muholi had co-founded, and the Joint Working Group, weighed in on the fray, defending Muholi's right to exist as an artist, commenting on the manner in which "gender variant" bodies are among the most-policed by government departments and asking questions about Xingwana's own extension of this violent policing to the terrain of Arts and Culture.

> FEW noted:
> [o]ur progressive Constitution [...] enshrines and protects the rights of lesbian, gay, bisexual and transgender (lgbt) people as well as the right to freedom of expression. Zanele Muholi is an internationally recognised artist who has extensively documented the everyday experiences of black lesbians. Her work has also focused attention onto the issue of hate crimes directed against black lesbians in South Africa. [...] Although Minister Xingwana is entitled to her personal opinion, as a representative of the government, we expect her to honour the equality clause in the Bill of Rights of our Constitution which protects diversity including LGBT rights. By walking out and expressing her outrage that this is immoral and unacceptable she is fuelling hostility against black lesbians. It is these same homophobic attitudes which motivate hate crimes. These are the very attitudes that FEW is working hard

to eradicate so as to build an inclusive society based on respect and tolerance of diversity.

I have quoted from FEW's and Gender DynamiX's statement in some length because they shift the debate as espoused in much of the media coverage to focus on specific prevailing discourses on gendered bodies. They do so in ways that are useful for my discussion here. In the excerpt, Xingwana's behaviour elicits a response from FEW on various, *interconnected*, levels. First, FEW argues that Xingwana's behaviour is at odds with the Constitutional provisions which protect both "freedom of expression" and "LGBT rights". Xingwana's exit positions her in relation to both of these. Second, FEW contests Xingwana's evaluation of Muholi's photographs as "not art" by citing the validation of the international artist community of Muholi's work as particularly outstanding art. Third, FEW reminds Xingwana that her participation – and therefore her response – happened in her capacity as an elected government official and such behaviour cannot then be protected as private opinion. Finally, FEW categorically refutes the separation between benign erasure of sexual expression and its more violent forms, by arguing that both exist along the same continuum. Xingwana does not need to enact hate crimes because her institutional location means that she has the power to sanction it from a distance. FEW refuses to recognise this distance or underlines the danger of this ostensible distance. When a Minister acts as Xingwana has chosen to, she provides institutional backing to the powerful "attitudes which motivate hate crimes". This stance by FEW rejects Xingwana's distancing from "tendencies that undermine the rights of people", her claims that she continues to "accept and respect the rights of people of different sexual orientation" as well as her insistence that she has "not imposed censorship on any artists".

Unlike Baderoon and Christiansë, among others, who foreground the slippery slope between Xingwana's pronouncements and censorship, FEW's statement suggests that censorship is not the only way in which harm can be done by one as powerfully located as Xingwana. Pronouncements that *attempt* to silence matter too.

Linking with FEW's statement, Gender DynamiX noted that

> [s]he is a government minister and so in condemning it outright, she claims that the entire nation echoes her opinion. It most certainly doesn't, as recent responses in the *City Press*, the *Times*, etc. clearly show. "Nation building", according to our very fine constitution, includes lesbians, transgender, gender non-conforming people, and so on – and it certainly includes artists. The constitution even has room for reactionary and conservative opinions like Xingwana's – but not as our national representative of arts and culture in this country and worldwide.

While Xingwana may have personal dislike for the artwork she saw, this organisation points to her position as a Minister in a democratically elected government with a progressive Constitution. This is done to show that her opinion is more than just that espoused by a citizen; it takes on institutional power by virtue of her position as a government official. These responses also argue that Xingwana's stance is part of a larger contradiction between the legislative framework of a democratic South Africa and the practice of government officials.

Both FEW and Gender DynamiX highlight how Xingwana's institutional location enacts a certain power whether or not she *personally* holds certain views. Both NGO statements also shift attention away from intention and personal biography of the Minister to effects of her actions given the office she holds.

FEW was "horrified" by Xingwana's response to "Zanele Muholi's photographs of lesbian couples", and the same remarks pique then columnist and senior journalist, Phylicia Oppelt's curiosity. Before she sees the photographs, she expects to find "the epitome of licentious vileness", but knows that no matter what the photographs contain, the nation Xingwana defends is not Oppelt's. Responding to the heteronormative social cohesion evoked by Xingwana, Oppelt declares:

But whose nation was Xingwana talking about? The one that is a perfect heterosexual construct comprising mommies and daddies, girlfriends and boyfriends, men and women, husband and wife, Adam and Eve?

Oppelt's comments rhyme with comments by many other feminist commentators who weighed in on the fray, highlighting the double standards contained in Minister Xingwana's stance. Oppelt emphasises the diverse gender and sexual spectrum lived by those who belong to the national collective she desires and claims; contrasting this continuum of gender and sexual expression to the limited version evoked by Xingwana's statement.

It is worth noting that although Xingwana's comments generated much commentary on the pages of mainstream and art media, very few of these comments paid attention to the artworks themselves. Oppelt is among a few Black feminist commentators who paid attention to the actual artworks exhibited, not just the larger political implications of the disagreement. In the main, much ink was spilt specifically on Xingwana's stance on Muholi, and considerably less on Mntambo's work exhibited in the same show. Furthermore, while Xingwana's statements elicited strong criticism and many came to the defence of the artists in question, very little critical engagement had been forthcoming at the time of the exhibitions. Indeed, the only references to the exhibitions, apart from announcements, that I could find in key art sites or by significant art critics referred to the controversy. These were not preceded by any engagement with the artworks, and where they made reference to the artists, they did so in biographical format with scant attention to the artworks (these were Sean O'Toole, the art magazine *Artthrob*, Peter Machen). Although Anthea Buys lists ten of her favourite women artists and includes Muholi and Mntambo in 2008, she does not mention the exhibition which opens in the same month as this list a year later, until the Xingwana controversy erupts, and in her piece she pays scant attention to Muholi's artwork, mainly to describe what it is not, and none to Mntambo. Art journalist, Mary Corrigal's review is a notable exception in hastily discussing some of Mntambo's work, but even she pays no attention to the other artists on display due to her stated irritation with women-themed exhibitions, three of which she rushes over in her review.

The art world's total silence on the exhibition is both symptomatic of Black artists' reception in contemporary South Africa, and a missed opportunity to interrogate key and varied Black feminist artwork that attempted to push our thinking on gender and embodiment. It is to some of the artworks included in *Innovat1ve Women* that I now turn. Space constraints dictate that I select some artworks rather than perform a careful reading of all the works on show.

Here, I choose to analyse the "offending" pieces by Mntambo and Muholi, but also make references to works by Masondo, Marasela and Shadi. The five are chosen because they all represent different spaces within the repertoire of Black women's embodiment that I argue Ms Xingwana – and many of her critics – failed to engage with. While each of the artists' works offers enough material for a full length paper on its own, I read Muholi and Mntambo both contextually through other Black feminist artists' work on show in the same space. It is important to note that various arguments can be made with reference to the omitted artworks as well.

Masondo's cheeky bodies

Ingrid Masondo's four photographic prints on archival paper are rendered in similar style across photographs but they evoke divergent associations; we cannot avoid asking questions about her visual language and subjects. Eschewing clear visual representation, Masondo's preference here is evocation and suggestion. With captivating use of colour, the movement and placement of her objects/bodies makes it difficult to categorically name what we are looking at. Her artistic decisions suggest that we need to consciously make use of varied sites of meaning: the naming of her photograph, the associations evoked by the visual images we encounter as well as that which her dolls and figures gesture towards.

'Solace' contains a smiling wooden doll, with an attached feather and explosions of colour. In 'Flight', we see another figure with an affixed feather. Both photographs use dolls and feathers, rendered in a matching colour palette, but that is where the similarity ends. In 'Flight' the body is turned away as though in dance, so that it is not immediately clear that the figure is not human, but a doll. This image suggests the dual meanings of "flight": fleeing and/as flying, both of which are supported by the presence of a feather.

The two remaining photographs juxtapose ambiguity with deliberate attention to detail. Consequently, the partially visible red leather item comes into view with a toy bus and doll superimposed on it in 'The Breadwinner' and it reappears as container for an equally unclear black article in 'Consternation'. The fine stitching on the red leather and attached cowrie shells evince deliberate attention to detail and ornamentation. Further, although we assume that the doll is the "breadwinner", she is a marionette with strings controlled by an invisibilised force. Masondo's work negotiates these apparent contradictions of uncertainty and deliberate choice, carefulness and attention to detail. At the same time, our inability to reach closure forces us to explore more abstract meanings.

In this manner, the artist invites us to ponder the location of power and control in the lives of women who work to support their families as breadwinners. The doll is a puppet, suggesting that she does not have full power to live her life as she pleases, shuttling, as she does, by packed bus in order to ensure the survival of others. At the same time, there is much power/agency in being a breadwinner and working productively to support her family.

Masondo's photographs hint at many layered contexts which cannot be contained within a frame, but which indelibly shape what is within it. In this manner, she forces us to reflect as much on what we see as what has been erased or obscured. While Masondo's images hold the eye with their explosion of reds, oranges and yellows against a recurrent glossy black backdrop, her images grab the eye but refuse to offer certainty. Instead, the artist juxtaposes the distorted and highlighted, producing connections and disjuncture to form a feminist strategy that calls authority into question.

The explosions of colour are eye-catching and the viewer is likely to allow her eye to linger longer on the beauty of the juxtaposition of bold colours in movement. The artist's refusal to provide certainty about what is within the frame, coupled with meanings that are gestured to but which lie beyond the borders of the photographs on display clash somewhat with the enchanting play of colour, crispness and blurring. The physical beauty of the work entices the viewer to dwell on the meeting places between pleasure and pain in women's lives, and specifically as these are played out in the relationship between "burden"/"glory" or erasure/mythologisation.

Masondo's work reminds us of the manner in which these patriarchal inscriptions – cast as binaries – are, in fact, imbricated, mutating positions and ideologies. For example, a character in Zoë Wicomb's 2000 novel, *David's Story*, reflects on this entanglement. Rachel, who is a former activist and MK combatant, reflects on the manner in which Black women's agency is only celebrated when it is in service of more than themselves. She notes,

> [d]ignity, it seemed, meant a bundle of dreary things for a woman: she had to keep her head covered at all times, was not to throw it back with laughter even in private, and above all, was not to venture outdoors after sunset without an escort.

The remainder of the time, sanctioned representations and/or performances of the location "Black woman" are limiting, as is clear in the reflection of another of Wicomb's characters from the same novel, mythologised Rain Sister, Antjie: "as if this burden disguised as an honour did not weigh heavily on her heart". In Masondo's photographs, viewers are forced to reflect on this connection between what is celebrated about women and what oppresses them.

At the same time, Masondo's photographs suggest that creative ways of rethinking how we name and represent women offer the possibility of new forms of being, and of things meaning differently.

Shadi's knotty becoming

If Masondo's photographs are an invitation to explicitly use our imaginations as a way to interpret creative works, Lerato Shadi's performance, 'Exposed pupa' startles in both its naming and various significations. In this performance piece, the artist's body is wrapped in a white cotton sheet with her head, neck and arms exposed, pulled from side to side.

Shadi's choice of name for this performance piece evokes both metaphoric and bodily transformation. As a pupa transforms itself into a butterfly, it also moves from the protective corporeal cocooning to flight. This artwork hints at the duality of associations with flight: the freedom that comes with flying movement as well as the implication of fleeing.

Sticking with the second meaning of flight, rather than protect her, the cocoon is unravelling and the pupa's transformation is a site of strife in place of graceful growth. Shadi's 'Exposed pupa' presents the artist's body as both performer and text to be made sense of. Unsettling, the performance also conjures up associations of crucifixion, as Shadi appears with exposed face, shoulder-length hair and outstretched arms in a moment of suffering.

Breaking with commonsensical understandings of pupae as a safe stage prior to full beautiful metamorphosis, Shadi's performance reminds us that all transformation is uncomfortable. It requires breaking down and/as growth. The associations with crucifixion connect physical and psychic – although not necessarily religious – alteration. Unlike traditional pupae, which are immobile and concealed both by placement as well as the casing, Shadi must grow in the full glare of the public with the transformation as struggle, rather than affirmation. Shadi's intertwining of possibility and pain also suggests something elusive about the suffering that can be the underbelly of beauty since her performance also contains suggestions that she is trapped and pained by her creation.

'Exposed pupa' contains an invitation to reflect on the process by which things become taken for granted because the protective state of growth is also a time of embattlement. Like Masondo's photographs discussed above, 'Exposed pupa' contains the uncomfortable reminder that ways of looking are selective.

When Xingwana walked out because she was affronted by Muholi's and Mntambo's artworks, she relegated the artistry of the remaining eight Blackwomen to the realm of the unimportant. Yet, both Masondo's and Shadi's work interrogate these very contradictions, slippages, power of creativity and its conditions of consumption.

Of bulls and tradition: self-insertion in Mntambo's art

Nandipha Mntambo contributed three artworks to the exhibition: 'Babel', which I will not discuss here, as well as 'The Rape of Europa' and 'Narcissus'. All three draw on Mntambo's recognisable signature of physical and metaphoric material from the bovine world to craft a deliberate commentary on the layering of place, wealth, language, sexuality and identities.

In 'The Rape of Europa' and 'Narcissus', the artist inserts herself into the frame – as both horned, furry aggressor minotaur (Zeus) and smooth-skinned violated (Europa) in the former ('The rape of Europa'), and as the incurably vain, hairy and horned narcissist, in the latter ('Narcissus'). Her corporeal integration complicates these narratives by introducing an internal opposition, rather than a discernible external power struggle. The setting for both is an idyllic Garden of Eden. The first work is also an intertextual reworking of Titian's sixteenth-century painting of the same name, where Zeus (in the form of a white bull) kidnaps Europa, a Phoenician nymph which could have been inspired by Ovid's *Metamorphosis*, as Donald Stone suggests, or "a princess with demi-god status" in Michael Wintle's reading. Titian's painting, "highly praised for its luminous colors and sensual textures", nonetheless "eroticizes rape", as suggested by AW Eaton, and echoed by Margaret Carroll.

'The Rape of Europa' was one of the artworks singled out by Xingwana as distasteful. With specific reference to this artwork, the Minister noted:

> [u]pon arrival at the Exhibition, I immediately saw images which I deemed offensive. The images in large frames were of naked bodies presumably involved in sexual acts. I was particularly revolted by an image called "Self-rape", depicting a sexual act with a nature scene as the backdrop. The notion of self-rape trivialises the scourge of rape in this country.

From this excerpt of the Minister's statement, it would appear that the photograph offers an assortment of insults. First the hypervisibility of copulating bodies brought into sharp focus such that they are difficult to miss in their "large frames" is disturbing. Secondly, Xingwana's misnaming of 'The Rape of Europa' as 'Self-rape' is revealing: it contradicts her claim that she was not aware of the gender of those within Mntambo's and Muholi's frames. She clearly recognised that the "rapist" and the "raped" were the same person and gender. She may also recognise that this figure is Mntambo, herself. Consequently, given the alarming figures of gender-based violence, and within that specifically rape, the idea of self-rape seems to insult those who experience the violence of rape. At the same time, the misnaming also demonstrates that Xingwana does not, in fact, mis-recognise what Mntambo seeks to do. Xingwana's objection is not premised on her failure to understand that rape is used metaphorically here. It is an objection to precisely rape's use as metaphor when most South Africans experience it as a violent act.

For Xingwana, then, it is clear Mntambo uses rape as a metaphor for a non-coherent self, and indeed an embattled self. This problematic metaphoric use is what Mary Corrigall picks up on when she analyses this image:

> [b]ecause Mntambo is both victim and perpetrator of the rape, she is engaged in a self-destructive act. This is not to say that the photograph implies that women are willing victims of rape, but perhaps that they too readily assume the victim role and in the process become agents of their own destruction.

Corrigall's reading of Mntambo, written long before the furore and as part review of the original exhibition, gives credence to Xingwana's resistance noted above. This is because Corrigall also reads into Mntambo's photograph some complicity by women in the status they assume in relation to rape. In other words, reading Corrigall cited immediately above, the difference between women's collusion with rape ("being willing victims of rape") and complicity in rape through their responses to it in its aftermath ("too readily assume the victim role and in the process become agents of their own destruction") is quite thin, even though Corrigall presents these as clearly different stances. Whether women elicit rape or behave inappropriately in response to its occurrence are both part of the same patriarchal script that trivialises the layered violation that is rape. There is very little difference between arguing that rape is something women are complicit in (what Xingwana suggests Mntambo implies, and Corrigall disputes in Mntambo), or "just sexual intercourse" to which women overreact (which is suggested in Corrigall as the more fitting interpretation of Mntambo). If we read rape to be both a physical and psychic/emotional violation, then it matters little where women's culpability is placed, quite contrary to what Corrigall argues.

Gail Smith partly concurs with Corrigall's reading when she stresses the importance of reading the metaphoric meanings of rape in relation to mediated self. Smith points out that Xingwana's misnaming of Mntambo's work is echoed in the Minister's misreading of the photographs. Smith notes that the images have less to do with rape as the violence experienced in many people's lives and more to do with metaphoric rape as conflictedness, introspection and coming to terms with parts of the self that are easier to disavow. While Corrigall and Smith are correct to point to the metaphoric meanings and uses of rape in Mntambo's art, Xingwana too shares this recognition. However, unlike them she refuses to accept the established use of rape as metaphor as an innocent act. Writing specifically of transhistorical deployment of rape in works of the imagination, and specifically within the visual art tradition, Emiliano Buis cautions:

> [t]he general inequality that lies at the basis of rape in myth is noticeable if one takes into account that most of the times the male god acting with aggressive impulse presents himself metamorphosed into a brute: This is the case of mighty Zeus attacking Europa as a bull, Leda as a swan, or Persephone as a snake; Poseidon as a bull raping Canace or as a dolphin forcing Melantho, and Apollo as a snake and a tortoise acting against Dryope. According to the mythical versions, these confused girls are usually placed in lonely environments lacking protection and where they will not be discovered right away.

From Buis, then, the metaphoric use of rape in fine art fails to mask the violence of rape whether material or imagined. In other words, the violence remains in the representation of rape. Such codification of violence is evident in the refusal of many art masters to represent the rapist in recognisable human or deity face – which at other times can be venerated. Indeed, the very act of rape is only conceivable as "artistic" when it is doubly mythologised: in the insistence that it be read exclusively as metaphor and in its distancing of the rapist into non-human form. This reading is supported by the tradition within which Mntambo provocatively locates herself – and her recognisable body – at the same time that she undermines it. This disruptive potential of Mntambo's work shows up more of what Corrigall will not engage when the latter of the two insists:

> Take Nandipha Mntambo's The Rape of Europa (2009), a highly stylised image which sees the artist posing as the defenceless and

nubile Europa and her rapist Zeus (disguised as a bull). This work articulates themes and ideas that extend beyond her identity as a black female. In assuming the roles of both Europa and the bull, Mntambo subverts what could have been a dialogue between the self and the other into a discourse with the self and divergent aspects of the self. In this way, Mntambo is both aggressor and victim, male and female, coloniser and colonised. Given that she tries to shirk fixed notions of identity through this work, it seems ironic that it would find its way to an exhibition that pigeonholes her as a black woman. Mntambo also engages and challenges Western myths and how its pervasive influence shapes one's concept of self.

This analysis is restricted at various levels. First, the mere exploration – indeed, recognition – of duality does not undo hierarchy. Therefore, even if Mntambo represents the polarity that Corrigall notes above: male/female, coloniser/colonised and aggressor/victim, it is also important to note what readings and meanings she engenders through this opposition.
As Melissa Steyn and Mikki van Zyl (2009) note

> *the desired* and *the desirable* are constructed through the simultaneous constellation of the *undesired* and *the undesirable*, deeply knotted into our gender, 'race', age, class and our times and place – integral and complex parts of our sense of self, or where and how we fit into the world. (italics in original)

This insight by Steyn and van Zyl illuminates two aspects of my argument here. First, it points to the limitations in Corrigall's conception of Mntambo's exploration of duality. The opposites listed in Corrigall are not just conflictual, they are also entangled. Second, Steyn and van Zyl's argument illustrates the struggle that Mntambo portrays. The intertextuality of her piece at once speaks to her own (embodied, historical and artistic) place and the will to disrupt the various traditions that seek to contain her. Reading her larger oeuvre, Mntambo returns to the meanings of bulls specifically across history and cultures to provoke, unsettle and re-inscribe them. At the same time, her impulse to insert her recognisable self into the frame in both 'Narcissus' and 'The Rape of Europa' unsettles the masking necessary for the art traditions in which she is located. This bodily self-insertion is a recognised feminist artistic strategy that problematises both the absence of women in certain kinds of conceptions of artistic genius and subverts the meanings of women's bodies in the fine arts tradition. This is achieved through the juxtaposition of desired aspects of art-making along with disruptive strategies.

Juxtaposition invites comparison; it is not unproblematic co-existence. Intertextuality is not just citation and historical reference. The strategic usefulness of intertextuality and juxtaposition are highlighted in Mntambo's self-insertion into the world of meanings. As Mary Orr reminds us, intertextuality's etymology does not only take us back to Julia Kristeva's coinage in the 1960s, but to the "extensive cultural re-appraisal" of several concepts, among them,

> (1) a unified self (especially a male subject position in hierarchical structures of knowledge and power); (2) the pre-eminence of high-cultural expression (as essentially white, male and European); and (3) direct referential connections between language and the world.

The questioned unified self has already been established in reference to Mntambo's artwork above, since this is one of the areas of consensus in the commentaries. The assumed direct connection between Mntambo's (or anybody's) visual language is undermined by the contestation over the meanings suggested in her artwork. The art tradition within which she is located, and which she interrogates through her intertextual and feminist strategies, is one that collates the knowing, authoritative, empowered artist as male, European and white. Quite contrary to what Corrigall argues above, then, the artworks on display highlight that it matters that Mntambo is a Black woman artist.

Second, "ideas that extend beyond her identity as a black female" are not necessarily ideas outside of her being a Blackwoman in the first place. In other words, to say that Mntambo's artwork resonates beyond topics linked to Black women subjects is not the same as saying that the fact of her being a Blackwoman is irrelevant to her art. Corrigall is unable to imagine identifying as a Blackwoman in ways that are not pigeonholing and limiting, even when she is confronted with an image that shows precisely how this position can be imagined, theorised and played with in non-pigeonholing ways. The existence of specifically Black feminist agency missed by Corrigall is not just in the photographs, but in the artist's extra-textual assertion as well. Mntambo, the artist in question, *chooses* to partake in this exhibition of Blackwomen about being a Black woman artist.

Twenty years before this exhibition, Kimberlé Crenshaw published a much-cited argument in which she theorised intersectionality as that which other feminist strands have also characterised as the multiple inflections of gender. Crenshaw conceived of intersectionality as that which would methodologically enable us to think beyond either/or and be able to see the multiple, coinciding and sometimes competing meanings at the same time. She also conceived of it specifically to think about Blackwomen and violence. Crenshaw noted that intersectionality "highlights the need to account for multiple grounds of identity when considering how the social world is constructed". Thinking through intersectionality allows us to see that Mntambo's artwork is simultaneously a very specific theorisation of Black women's location in art tradition (this tradition both frames and alienates her), a crafting of a Black feminist visual language (through refusal to self-mask using the same European patriarchal mythologised), making different decisions about what can and cannot be seen. Her body and commentary suggests both that she claims her space as art genius *and* recasts the conditions of her location by refusing blind incorporation. To the extent that all creative production is always about the specific that also has wider relevance, Mntambo's work is about *both* aspects "beyond" being a Blackwoman and very specifically about being a Blackwoman. Intersectionality enables a reading of this complexity rather than an investment in a binaristic reading of either one or the other.

Muholi's visual traditions

Zanele Muholi's project both connects with and departs from Mntambo's. In five silver gelatine and Lambda prints, the artist invites us to reflect on issues of self-representation alongside those of spectatorship. As I have argued elsewhere, Muholi's treatment of lesbian self-hood is both historicised and forward looking in visual languages that enfold her subject matter. In the photographs 'Musa Ngubane and Mabongi Ndlovu, Hillbrow, Johannesburg, 2007', and 'Julia and "Mandoza" Hokwana, Lakeside, Johannesburg, 2007' two couples are rendered in stylised gendered portraiture. Here, Muholi tinkers with the varied registers of performed femininities and masculinities by Black lesbians in Johannesburg. The spectator may interpret the poses and Muholi's subjects, based on recognition of the format of heterosexual domestic portraiture: a man in upright, stiff pose either standing alongside a chair on which a less stiff woman sits, or himself sitting equally stiffly in a chair with a standing woman leaning into his body. The foregrounded figure in this tradition is the man. The portraits of the couples rendered in these two photographs by Muholi both invite recognition of this tradition and subvert the expectations of such portraiture. In both photographs, we are presented with Black lesbian couples. As in other places in her larger opus, Muholi toys with expectation: inviting recognition in order to introduce something startling. The highly circulated genre of photographic portraiture is undermined by who is in the frame rather than who is referenced.

In her 2007 triptych, 'Being', the embracing or spooning couples' hips are wrapped in a single beige mesh scarf in one photograph and in plastic cling wrap in another. This triptych is in conversation with hegemonic representations of (Black) lesbians. The women within the frame are versions of venerated Black femininity: attractive, small bodied, with trendy hairstyles whether flowing weaved hair or close-cropped uncombed hairstyles. These women embody the kind of physical beauty celebrated in women's magazine advertisements and advice content. In such magazines, women who look like this are assumed heterosexual and rendered safe for consumption through a heterosexual gaze and an entitled heteropatriarchal male gaze.

Muholi photographed these couples in the manner of fashion and cosmetic shoots so beloved of women's magazines. They are familiar, and yet unlike the models from these familiar photographs, Muholi's couples do not perform for the camera. It is the camera that intrudes. The cling wrap suggests two oppositional meanings. First, it is a critique of regimes through which women's intimacy is packaged for a heterosexist audience that is titillated by what has been codified as "girl-on-girl" action, at the same time as acting violently to real-life lesbians. Second, the cling wrap is a nod to the varied uses of plastic in the performance of lesbian desire and pleasure. In each case the women's bodies or women subjects turn towards each other to show "engaging, evocative images of intimacy between two women", as McKaiser's 2010 response to Xingwana recognises.

Muholi's photographs here, and elsewhere, are meticulously focused on ways of seeing where Black lesbian lives are concerned, posing the question of "what do you see when you look at me?". Her work is simultaneously attentive to the quotidian Black lesbian experience, violence and erasure of Black lesbian subjectivity, and highlighting the joy and beauty of Black lesbian desire. It is interesting that Xingwana sees stereotype in Muholi and Mntambo and the absence of an interrogation of Black women's representation. The Minister's statement does not elaborate on which stereotypes were evoked, making it difficult to focus specifically on which strategies she found questionable.

In place of the horror suggested by Xingwana's comments, Oppelt discovers in Muholi's photographs "images of naked women curled around and into each other [....] I liked the emotional warmth in the photographs, the ordinariness of their bodies, the tenderness that emanates from Muholi's work." Oppelt's recognition of "naked vulnerability" of Muholi's subjects, "emotional warmth", and "the ordinariness" of the bodies clashes with Xingwana's relegation of the same artworks to the realm of pornography and stereotype. Both pornography and stereotype are oppressive, limiting forms of representation, which enact violence on the displayed bodies as well as inviting a complicit gaze from the audience.

Interestingly, Oppelt locates Xingwana's problem within the realm of looking differently. Xingwana has "blinkers" here, just like Baderoon would later write of Xingwana's overly hasty glance. Visual scholars have long theorised the manner in which looking is ideological. Film theorist, Laura Mulvey's ground-breaking theorisation of the male gaze illustrated the manner in which ways of looking both enact and are implicated in patriarchal power. John Berger demonstrated how ways of looking and seeing can be learnt and naturalised across time. This influences as much what we regard as art as it does what we turn away from.

In other words, Oppelt, McKaiser, Smith and Baderoon see the limitations in Xingwana's cursory glance which denies the Minister the opportunity to recognise the strategies used in the artwork she dismisses. Her quick glance or "blinkers" prevent her from moving beyond the "recognition" aspect of juxtaposition and intertextuality central to readings of both Muholi's and Mntambo's very different visual repertoires.

Marasela's staged recall

Black women's subjectivity is interrogated and imagined in yet another direction in the photographs by Senzeni Marasela included in Bengu's show. Marasela's photographs also bear traces of intertextuality with citations of older, recognisable traditions of seeing Black bodies in the South African city, and specifically in Johannesburg. Her work weaves in and out of various traditions fusing visual referents from venerated and marginalised urban languages about Black bodies.

In four photographic prints on archival paper, Senzeni Marasela presents a familiar figure, Theodora, from her 2005 'Theodora and other women', while partly referencing her 2000 'Our Mother'.

Theodora is recognisable in two senses: as a recurring character in Marasela's work, and, because of her clothing, the familiar Blackwoman as domestic worker.

In 'Theodora comes to Johannesburg, Inside an old shop in Klipspruit', Theodora occupies the centre of the frame physically and metaphorically. She is what matters, as clear from the naming of the photograph and the series it belongs to. Surrounded by old walls, with broken green glass and stones on the dirty cement floor, she is in an abandoned building. The old shop has started to disintegrate with peeling cement and paint. The writing on the wall, in different handwritings, is a nod to the diverse times and agents of the inscriptions. Klipspruit was created in 1905 to contain Black labour away from the city centre, like many townships in what would become Soweto. In this photograph, both Theodora and Klipspruit are markers of histories of Black labour in the city.

In all the photographs, Theodora has turned away from the camera so the viewer has no access to her feelings, expressions, or other facial specificities. Here Marasela's work continues on her previous mnemonic engagements with apartheid and previous histories, as the scholars Mark D'Amato and Lauri Firstenberg 2002 might suggest, including legacies of documentation. Whereas critics of Marasela's work have highlighted the artist's concerns with anthropological and photographic documentaries, the naming of the current Theodora series suggests further inter-textual play. The repeated 'Theodora comes to Johannesburg' echoes and revisits the familiar 'Jim comes to Joburg' narratives.

After Donald Swanson's 1949 film of the same name, the latter became shorthand for narratives which portrayed "naïve" Blackmen from villages who came to Johannesburg in search of the idyllic life associated with the city of gold. Upon arrival, Jim finds the reality much harsher, but as he adapts to the new setting, he is rewarded with gradual success.

Marasela's 'Theodora comes to Johannesburg' series is more than a rewriting of this script to insert a Blackwoman's presence in the city. Rather than a revision, these photographs invite us to reflect on the many simultaneous presences that have shaped the spaces Theodora visits. Discovery and disillusion are interwoven ways of being: supplementary, mutually constitutive and adjacent. Theodora's crisp yellow, coordinated outfit is sharply contrasted with her decaying surroundings. Her dress, doek and flat black shoes are signs of agency, hinting at deliberate choice and alerting us to her specific tastes that are not immediately related to the scenes she visits. She may be a Blackwoman in the ruins of Klipspruit, but she is also much more. The artist reminds us that to see/recognise Theodora does not translate into unmediated access to her interiority. While Blackwomen like Theodora are familiar, they perform multiple subjectivities which cannot be contained by their contextualisation and recognition as a "type". Gabeba Baderoon theorises a similar agency as a "leaking of meanings" in her poetry.

Theodora's yellow is bright and hopeful and in all the photographs her face is illuminated, unlike the death of hope suggested by her physical environment. Always presented with her back turned, she is not entirely available for view, interpretation and knowledge. She may be partly representative, but even the function of such representativeness is questioned. In 'Theodora comes to Johannesburg, shop in Klipspruit', she stands in the doorway, on her way elsewhere, away from the walls inscribed with "Ek het klaar gelag" and "Trust no one".

Here, memory is used as both a historical engagement and as an invitation to imagine. Such pasts remain a haunting, in the sense that Patricia Williams evokes, always embedded in the present. This interpretation is brought into particularly sharp focus in the final photograph in the series, 'Theodora comes to Johannesburg, The Turbine Hall in Newtown', which has large windows through which skyscrapers can be seen; one wall is lined with blue bins.

Turbine Hall opens up different possibilities from the other dilapidated places Theodora has walked through. The neatly lined blue bins hint at a building that is not another abandoned, forgotten space. This site offers the possibility of rejuvenation, linking memory to the imagined future, as do the various photographs included by this artist for this exhibition. They all offer reminders of a memory, with echoes, recognition and elision.

spaces of engagement

As I wrap up this reflection, I turn to the work of two feminists whose work has been critical in interrogating how we think about feminist imagination in different locales. First, Elaine Salo reminds us that

> [m]ultiple shifts have occurred in women's struggles in South Africa, and they have had to invent equally multiple and innovative strategies and spaces of engagement, as well as enter into new alliances with other gendered movements to effect gender justice.

Second is Margaret Atwood's insistence that

> [t]he tendency of innovative literature is to include the hitherto excluded, which often has the effect of rendering ludicrous the conventions that have preceded the innovation.

Innovat1ve Women rose to the very difficult task of reflecting on existing ways of knowing at the same time as being inventive. Collectively these artworks offer a refreshing vision of the diverse meeting places of the imagination, power and play. In a world with competing prescriptive declarations of what is known and knowable, these artists value ways of questioning, provoking and unsettling the conventional. In diverse ways, these artists offer startling clarity of vision and offer a glimpse of the remarkable genius of Blackwomen artists working in South Africa today.

This combination of violence, play and beauty is revisited by all the artists in this show in markedly different registers. Individually and collectively, these Blackwomen artists suggest a different visual languaging of Blackwomen's artistic agency and subjectivities as complex. "Innovative women" have to recognise and create at the same time. In other words, they have to reflect on what exists while breaking new ground.

Ingrid Masondo achieves this in her use of unclear, blurred objects rendered in captivating colourscapes. Consequently, we are drawn into what she portrays even if she never affords us the certainty of knowing exactly what physical objects we are looking at. Her photographs are provocative and transformative of the gaze due in no small measure to her commitment to uncertainty.

Lerato Shadi's captivating performance of growth in the full glare of an audience is both familiar and discomfiting. It is not just visually provocative but also unsettles the associations we have about what we see and what it means.

Nandipha Mntambo's questioning strategies are as provocative as they are playful. This artist draws on competing mythologies, resisting readings of binaries, with a clear preference for fusions, paradox and complexity rather than surrendering to tidy oppositional binaries. In highly varied registers, she plays with difference and discovery, even as she relies on recognition. In this way, attraction and repulsion are part of the same braided voice: eloquent, provocative and inventive.

Zanele Muholi's varied photographs explore different aspects of Black lesbian subjectivity. She makes clear choices about the photographs included in this exhibition. All are unapologetic in their concern with self and beloved: inward looking, intimate, turned into each other. She offers us different slices of the coupledom and domesticity marking Black lesbian: quotidian, record and intimacy.

Senzeni Marasela offers beautiful contrast and turns on its head what we think we know. Her photographs offer a familiar figure in famous places, yet they also remind us that "we" do not know "her". Instead, "we" have glimpses and there is much that the gaze cannot access regardless of what hegemonic constructions often suggest. Marasela chooses to "render ludicrous" such traditions of the knowable "maid" figure.

Together, these artists present a dynamic, refreshing and provocative vision of the range of ways in which Black feminist imagination works. It is testament to the stubbornness of hegemonic representations of Blackwomen in stereotypical guise that Xingwana cannot see the varied refreshing ways in which these artists revisit, interrogate and chart new ways of representing Blackwomen.

The range of possibilities in the artists selected for discussion here highlights how gender is always variously inflected, rather than restricted to unmoored meanings. The exhibition artworks deal with precisely the multitude of such inflections even when the producers of the artwork are similarly located as Black women artists in South Africa.

In my analysis, I have allowed the artworks themselves to theorise, while I have also borrowed from other feminist tools to further unlock meanings from select artworks exhibited in Bengu's show. While I recognise that all framing is selective – and that these artworks can exist in different exhibition spaces, collections and contexts – I have nonetheless demonstrated how Bengu's framing both highlights the specific Black feminist strategies used here and enables Baderoon's leaking of meanings.

Together – and separately – these artworks illustrate Salo's "equally multiple and innovative strategies and spaces of engagement", given that as Atwood says, feminism "has influenced how people read, and therefore what you can get away with, in art".

Here, I have also demonstrated the manner in which Black feminist contestation occurs not just against the context of Black/white patriarchy or white feminism, but the presence of internal disputes in conceptions of what constitutes Black feminist visual language. In Phylicia Oppelt's phrase, the differences between Xingwana – with a long history of gender-progressive activism – and the artists in *Innovat1ve Women* were "not merely a little storm in a lesbian teacup" but a staging of the very diverse senses of how to speak about gender, language and nation especially in relation to Black women's bodies in the nation.

CHAPTER 7

A Blackwoman's journey through three South African universities

> *The space I occupy might be explained by my history.*
> *It is a position into which I have been written. I am*
> *not privileging it, but I do want to use it. I cannot*
> *fully construct a position that is different*
> *from the one I am in.*
> — GAYATRI SPIVAK

Discussions on transformation have been foregrounded in the psyches of South African university communities since the early 1990s. While unevenness characterises the dispersal of transformation politics, all universities must be seen to engage with this process. Transformation has been about questioning the structure and business of South African universities with a view to bringing them in line with the Constitution of the Republic and the new era. Transformation has presented challenges since it requires an overhaul of universities in order to reshape them into spaces which demographically mirror the country's population while addressing specific needs for equity as stipulated under the Employment Equity Act, 1988 (Act 55 of 1998). Under this Act employees are required to identify and eliminate all employment barriers present in the work situation. The Act places emphasis on the experiences and representation of designated groups: Black people, women and the disabled. The Employment Equity Act's stipulations on equity are further affirmed in the Promotion of Equality and Prevention of Unfair Discrimination Act, 2000 (Act 4 of 2000). In addition to this, there are policies which concern themselves primarily with institutions of higher learning in South Africa, such as the *White Paper on Education and Training*, which stresses the need to initiate "measures of empowerment" and the 2001 National Plan for Higher Education, which aims, according to its Section 3, "[t]o ensure that the student and staff profiles progressively reflect the demographic realities of South African society [particularly with a view to] increase the representation of blacks and women in academic and administrative positions, especially at senior levels". A recent survey conducted by the National Research Foundation shows that women constitute 34 per cent of academic staff and that even those are located at the lower rungs of the university hierarchy.

This chapter traces my experiences at three different South African universities, which have played distinct roles in my life, as a way into an examination of the challenges facing equitable relations at the institutions at which I was previously employed, the University of the Free State, previously the University of the Orange Free State. It is particularly useful to consider that the three institutions I will be reviewing are classified differently in South African-speak on tertiary education. The University of Fort Hare is a Black university whereas the universities of Cape Town (UCT) and the (Orange) Free State are historically white institutions. The latter two are further differentiated by the politics that shaped the campuses in the past and continue to retain currency. The

University of Cape Town was characterised predominantly by liberal sentiment and political activity from both student and staff communities, where Orange Free State's identity was linked with conservative Afrikaner politics. My relationships and locations with these institutions are highly varied, and in their juxtaposition I hope to achieve a level of inter-institutional commentary. Although I have previously found myself immersed in all three contexts, this chapter will testify to the contrasting experiences opened up by the various institutional socio-political personalities. Further, reading the University of the Free State through my previous experiential location at Fort Hare and UCT ensures that my assumptions and expectation are made transparent.

Because of the low numbers of Black staff members of both genders at South African universities, a level of mystique surrounds the machinery of academic institutions. The fact that university communities are transient adds to this. For example, when the Makgoba affair erupted, the public response was partly surprise. This was and remains the case, even though some aspect of university politics is always in the news. The university, in the main, is perceived as an institution of which many are a part in preparation for the rest of their lives. The nature of undergraduate participation at university means that even for the most active students, much of the working of the institution remains shrouded in mystery.

The change in political dispensation has also contributed to confusion on how to counteract systems of oppression still in place. Faced with the ever-changing face of racism, Black people in contemporary South Africa have yet to target collectively and develop "new ways to talk about racism and other politics of domination", to quote bell hooks. Given a tradition of facing systems of oppression in familiar guise under apartheid, *public* challenges to the insidious ways in which institutions are still implicated in processes of racist capitalist patriarchy are few and far between. The resultant façade is of relative transformation at institutions of education.

This chapter does not depart from the same premise. To the extent that I have always been a part of a university community, in different guises, universities are not objects of intrigue. They are spaces I have woven myself into, and out of, and I continue to do so. Most studies on institutional culture focus on its inadequacies as far as equitable representation of Black people and/or women in the academic staff are concerned, or on the limited resources even when employed by universities. To the extent that universities are visible towers in/of knowledge production, the nature of this knowledge, or systems of knowledge, should be unpacked and subjected to scrutiny. This is particularly so given that power is institutionally defined.

The perspective of an insider in the academic world is a valuable lens for making sense of the politics of academic institutions. My central argument is that universities are intimately implicated in the reproduction of these systems of power. They are not the cerebral uncontaminated spaces they are believed to be. My examination of the politics of the University of the Free State is informed by this and demonstrates here how this system of politics permeates the university at all levels.

language and power

> Part of our struggle for radical black subjectivity is the struggle to find ways to construct self that are oppositional and liberatory
> – BELL HOOKS

My earliest memories of the University of Fort Hare are of black fists looming large against the white walls of Tyali 1 and 2, the male residence halls, which were close to the home in which I grew up. The Group Areas Act delineated specific living zones for South Africans depending on their racial classification. Black rural living areas and townships were usually an inconvenient distance away from their places of work so that travel to work was in itself strenuous. Several universities, among them Fort Hare, responded to the stipulations of this Act by offering accommodation to their staff members on the university campuses and on university property, which could not be regulated by the government to the same extent. What resulted was an "artificial" mix of languages and "races" on these campuses, which was out of step with the apartheid-legislated and constructed "norm" beyond the fences of the campuses. This is the kind of world into which I was born and inevitably Fort Hare was to influence my expectations and experiences of university life in myriad ways. Growing up on a university campus meant that I could perhaps not be the poster-child for South African Black children at the time. It also meant that by the time I went to school I was aware of the atypicality of our lives as well as the privileges this loophole in the aggressively degrading system of the day accorded my family.

Because I was born in the early seventies I was a child when the Black Consciousness ideology dominated Black university campus politics. While growing up, I was therefore surrounded by diversity and by a variety of Black male and female intellectuals, both situations which the apartheid government had discouraged by legislation. I was to have these people as role models I could see every day, a situation that was recognised as needed by Black children growing up, especially under apartheid.

The progressive Black magazine *Tribute,* which is now an institution in Black thought, saw this as the key to shaping Black minds of the future from the very onset when its subtitle/byline was 'A Tribute to Black Excellence'. If apartheid nourished itself on the doctrine of Black inferiority, bestiality and degeneracy, institutions which testified to the contrary were vital. Communities such as these attest to the fabrication and constructedness of naturalised discourses of racism: that Black people were meant for servitude and that "races" could not mix harmoniously.

In addition to this, student politics were vibrantly dynamic and defiance was a significant part of this era. Shouts of "Black Power" were commonplace, and this revolutionary slogan of Black affirmation was to be among my first phrases of initiation into the English language. As a child I was aware of the politics of the day, albeit vaguely, through overheard snippets of adult conversation. The connection between national politics and academic institutions was subtly communicated to me. It was also clear that the police, as organs of the apartheid state, were responsible for many of the physical disturbances on the campus and that they were not to be trusted. The lessons about the police, teargas and toyi-toying were, of course, not unusual socialisation for Black children in South Africa. Indeed, the violent and violating police presence was more pervasive in South Africa's sprawling townships. However, being born into a world in which Black Consciousness politics were the norm, into a middle-class home with two professional parents, with the oldest Black university on the African continent in modern times as my playground, meant that as a child I was to take for granted many aspects about Black life and the ability to access resources.

Fort Hare politics were to change over the years. I was to later realise the contradictions in the doctrine of Black Consciousness and study them. Black Consciousness went into decline and the politics of non-racialism/non-racism returned to centre stage. The Black Power salutes and fists waned, but the defiance and political militancy were to continue well into my early adulthood. The contrast between the violent politics of the day and the immaculate gardens of the Fort Hare campus are foremost in my mind. Even then, the university was a place from which multiple, sometimes conflicting, meanings flowed.

The Fort Hare of my childhood contrasts sharply with the Fort Hare of today. There are new challenges for Fort Hare – and indeed all Black institutions – in the new dispensation. No longer under physical or epistemic threat from state-sponsored violence, they are plagued by dwindling numbers, escalating debt because of student non-payment, as well as the challenges facing the general academic community nationally, including subsidy cuts.

language is power

As a young adult the first university I enrolled at was UCT. Here the public discourse was critical, but still limited by liberal politics that had first come under attack during the Black Consciousness phase in South Arica. Arriving at UCT in 1990, I was one of a small minority of Black students, which grew at a small pace throughout my years there. The liberal politics of the campus meant that I could participate openly in anti-racist and feminist student organisations in different capacities – ranging from supporting their activities, to being a member and sitting on steering or sub-committees.

As an undergraduate I found kinship with others who articulated similar ideological positions and was exposed to the theory behind them, even as I was aware that my introduction to the politics of race and gender had been shaped much earlier. This observation has been articulated elsewhere by Blackwomen of older generations in South Africa who were to later embrace Black feminist/womanist politics passionately, such as Ellen Kuzwayo, Emma Mashinini and Mamphela Ramphele. It was at UCT that I realised, through experiences that are sometimes contradictory, that I was neither insane nor alone in my desire to maintain a connection between and understanding of how race and gender work to inscribe separately as well as concurrently. It was here, at perhaps the most unlikely place, that I recognised explicitly that there were many others who felt as I did. Feeling this way at UCT was ironic, given the meaning of "liberal" in South African politics, where in left-wing discourses it is perceived as occupying a position at the centre of the spectrum. Progressive people associate liberalism with paternalistic attitudes towards Black people. Thus, to be liberal in South Africa does not mean to be open-minded or critical – except to liberals themselves. Black Consciousness activists had introduced the level of hostility directed at liberals, and indeed one of the uniting sentiments across the anti-racist student movement was the intense dislike for liberal politics. As an undergraduate student at UCT, I remember that the chant "Phantsi ngabelungu abasithandayo, phantsi!" or "Phantsi ngamaliberal, phantsi" when shouted at rallies, protest marches and political demonstrations was equally likely to come from the mouth of a South African National Students Congress (SANSCO, later SASCO), Pan Africanist Students Congress

(PASO) or Azanian Students Congress (AZASCO) sympathiser or member. In her essay, 'I was a white liberal and survived', Margaret Legum has noted that liberals in South Africa

> tend to use the words race prejudice, race discrimination and racism interchangeably, as though they mean roughly the same thing. This allows them, for instance, to equate job reservations against Africans with the formation of a black people's support group in a white organization, calling them both 'racist'. Superficially, there is a similarity; but everyone knows they are not equivalent – just as we know the killings committed by French Nazis are not normally equivalent to those committed by the Resistance [....] It follows that our actions as white liberals in opposing race discrimination do not exempt us from the effects of racism. To say that is to claim a place in *The Guiness Book of Records* as being the only people who have ever grown up without being affected by their culture.

While the numbers of Black students were very small in the early nineties, we were consciously a highly visible presence. We resisted narrow and constricting ways of representing Blackness and indelibly shaped the face of UCT socially and politically. While student politics was a vibrant and affirming arena, my experience of undergraduate academic work differed. With very few exceptions, I could not recognise myself in the UCT humanities curriculum. At this institution I was to identify lies and snatches about myself clearly in the course material. The fragments remained thus because the components that included me tended to be a small part of the general course. Even these were few and far between.

As an undergraduate the general air of criticism by the student body at UCT was one with which I fell in quite comfortably. I was often angry about how obvious it was to me that certain things were just not right. When Mamphela Ramphele, a former Black Consciousness activist, outspoken feminist campaigner and later the first Blackwoman to take office as vice-chancellor at a South African university, initiated a sexual harassment policy as then head of the Equity Unit, it was nothing short of revolutionary.

However, when this same policy was met with hostility from some Black male quarters whom I had considered comrades on campus, it was a stunning revelation. Pumla Gobodo-Madikizela, then a doctoral candidate in the Psychology Department at UCT, was to comment later on a slightly different incident, during which Ramphele was inscribed in similarly misogynistic ways by some Black male members at UCT: "What does a Black male chauvinist do to rally support from fellow Blacks, including women, against a Black woman seen as a threat – 'to the nation'? He invokes the notion of 'we-ness'. He casts himself into the role of custodian of culture."

Ramphele, a woman who always spoke her mind, inspired me, even as I was keenly aware of the insidious endeavours to silence such a Blackwoman. She was later to comment on the ways in which attempts to gag her took the forms of either labelling her "a mother or a cigarette smoking whore" in an interview with Mark Gevisser.

The contradictions of this space, with its anti-racist militancy and occasional flare-ups of misogyny, were obvious to me. Nevertheless, at UCT I was challenged to translate my anti-racist and feminist politics into practice. Through various discussions of anti-racist and feminist pedagogy with colleagues at the Academic Development Unit, I was able to launch a phase where I thought critically about the ways in which teaching can take place and to examine quite thoroughly how I would like to participate in the learning of my students – to embody a classroom practice that complemented rather than collided with my politics.

UCT managed to exist with its contradictions. Whereas the general public discourse encouraged and even invited critical questioning, in practice this behaviour was not welcome. As postgraduate student and tutor in the English Department, although this department "had participated in discussions about its role, its methods, its ideologies and its changes since the mid-1980s", according to Baderoon, the tenuous position I, as well as other postgraduate tutors, occupied in the department and the institution generally was apparent. As Baderoon has demonstrated, the "process of gradually becoming an insider reveals the crucial and at times uncomfortable power" of how language works to inscribe control and position. Thus, if first year students with whom they had contact in the tutorial system perceived tutors as the face of the university, I too was participating in this lie. The university, I felt, had not responded fast enough to the changes in student demographics. This was particularly ironic given that, to quote Baderoon, "[i]n the important recent review of the department's work which led to changes in the English 1 (and inevitably, other undergraduate) programmes, the views of the postgraduates were absent, though they did most of the English 1 tutoring until that time". Thus while this position was regarded by the institution as superfluous, it marked my initiation into the academic world of teaching and research, which would ultimately lead to full-time employment at another South African university. Gayatri Chakravorty Spivak demonstrates that my experience as a graduate tutor insider-outsider at the teaching establishment at UCT is not exceptional for post-colonial scholars. Speaking about this position as prevalent and linking it directly to her encounter in an interview published as 'The Postcolonial critic', she has noted:

> As far as I understand, in order to intervene one must negotiate. If there is anything I have learnt from the last 23 years of teaching, it is that the more vulnerable your position, the more you have to negotiate. We are not talking about discursive negotiations, or negotiations between equals, not even a collective bargaining. It seems to me that if you are in a position where you are [...] being constituted by Western liberalism you have to negotiate to see what positive role you can play from within the constraints of Western liberalism (which is a very broad term) breaking it open [...] you have to make interventions in the structure of which you are part, it seems to me that is the most negotiated position, because you must intervene even as you inhabit those structures.

When I finally left UCT I imagined that the lesson Spivak refers to was one I had learnt. When I arrived at the University of the Orange Free State, however, I was to put this understanding to a series of tests.

the languages of power

This is the attitude I brought with me to the University of the Orange Free State, as it was then called, in January 1997. However, teaching at this institution was to present serious challenges to my teaching style and personal politics. Before long I grasped that the atmosphere at the University of the Orange Free State was nothing like my previous one. Gone was the liberal pretence at equality and free speech and in its place, I soon realised, was a rigid regime, which declared that naming racism and sexism was forbidden. After my first lecture, which was an introduction to Black Consciousness literature, provoked protest from a right-wing student organisation, I was to question that adage commonly heard from Black South Africans about our preference for right-wingers who will tell us to our faces about their hatred of us, rather than the hypocritical smile and politeness for which liberals are known. In retrospect, I realise that the former is not a choice at all.

Although I received support from members of my department, the Dean proceeded as though the students in question had legitimate concerns, without discussing the matter with me even once. Thus, I felt undermined by the experience. Not once had I been called to the Dean's office to be notified of or asked to respond to these critiques from some of the students in my class. I was to realise that white supremacist patriarchy manifests itself in less hidden ways at the university. My desire and decision to name the situation as influenced by racist and misogynist thinking yielded even less satisfactory results for me. No breakthroughs were forthcoming.

This incident was one of many. The Faculty of Humanities audit, conducted by the faculty's equity committee (of which I am a member), yielded interesting, if unsurprising, results. According to the Employment Equity Act of 1998 each employer is required to identify barriers to equitable relations and optimum performance by their employees and then draft a programme through which the identified employment barriers will be addressed. The audits are to be particularly focused on how designated groups (i.e. Black people, women, disabled people) experience their workplace. The faculty audit was to eventually contribute towards a university-wide report to be submitted by the University of the Free State to the National Department of Labour.

I was acutely aware, as are most Black and/or women staff members in the faculty, of the scepticism about our ability to function as professionals. The audit revealed racial and sexual harassment to be rife. Black and/or women staff members were hesitant to offer critiques, for fear of being further victimised. It is telling that when specific cases of victimisation were mentioned, various staff members required that confidentiality be ensured. Also notable were the large number of doubts expressed by members of designated groups in the faculty about the possibility and pace of real transformation at both the faculty and university levels. It became clear when I spoke to several other colleagues from the designated groups that my experiences were neither unique nor the worst. These conversations also made it clear to me that, as Vanessa Persal says, "inequity does not have its most severe effect on our intellect – it destroys our dignity and self-esteem and these are experience of our 'self' – our psychosocial construct".

When this essay was first published, the remaining faculties were still engaged in the process of auditing their staff components. Our findings were not unique. The university proceeded for the duration of those audits as though the process of transformation was, even if agonising, at least guided and orderly.

The nature of student politics, however, contradicts this stated transformation. As part of the 2001 Student Representative Council (SRC) campaign, the Democratic Alliance (DA), the Here XVII and the de la Queillerienas mounted posters all over campus that declared language was a battleground. One of the posters screamed, "SLEGS ENGELS IS SLEGTER AS SLEGS BLANKES" which translates into "English only is worse than Europeans only", a reference to the amenities marked for exclusive white use in apartheid South Africa. These students see calls for greater accessibility to Afrikaans institutions as a threat to their language and culture. As the poster demonstrated, there is no recognition of the differences between oppressive past laws and initiatives to correct their effects on the present. This campaign is also insensitive to the apartheid reality that Black people have recently lived through, as well as the particularly brutal relationships Black people have with enforced participation in the Afrikaans-language context. Afrikaans-medium universities resist the language changes which will address this insidious past. At institutions such as the University of the Free State, which, according to the mission statement, uses a dual-medium system (English and Afrikaans), the bulk of the university's affairs continued to be conducted exclusively in Afrikaans. While lectures and tutorials are (theoretically) duplicated to allow students the choice of attending one in either language, reports of lecturers refusing to offer lectures and/or course material in English are not uncommon. In the main, correspondence with the university community, even confidential documents, are still written in Afrikaans. Challenges to this system, which are numerous, are met with blanket hostility, defensiveness, and tokenistic attempts at translating some documents for staff circulation. The experiences referred to by Black staff members of the Faculty of Humanities confirm this, as do sentiments expressed at the meetings of the Black Staff Forum.

The reactionary and absurd responses that equate apartheid and corrective measures are not unique to the university I was then employed by. Nor are the perfunctory attempts to dub the University of the Free State a university interested in using three languages in its operation because of its location in the Free State. SeSotho, officially the third language since the name change from the University of the Orange Free State to the University of the Free State/Universiteit van die Vrystaat/Yunivesithi yaFreistata in 2001, is used superficially in newsletters where it does not take up much space. These oversights remain because the national reconciliation and rainbow text deems that all South Africans are now equal, that injustices are a thing of the past that have minimal effect on contemporary interactions between South Africans on a daily basis. Unsurprisingly, as I have argued elsewhere,

> It becomes possible thus, hiding under rainbowism, to dismiss the effects of history on the contemporary, the need for affirmative action and black and/or women's empowerment initiatives. It reinforces the illusion of pervasive equality and negates the need for equity endeavours to rectify the effects of the interlocking systems of apartheid, patriarchy and capitalism among others.

The effects of rainbowist mythology as I argue in that same article and as Motsemme and Ratele have argued similarly about the reconciliation text, is that it erases difference and occludes the effects of history. In their repeated performance, rainbowism and reconciliation acquire the status of truth, so that reconciliation is seen to have been achieved and the rainbow nation seen as describing an existing reality. In this manner race difference assumes the status of non-entity, "so that ultimately white supremacy, which drove apartheid and remains institutional, albeit not state sponsored, racism, becomes a phenomenon which is whitewashed of all meaning". Consequently, white solipsism is left unquestioned, as the narrative pertaining to the "reconfiguration of power is retold in the past tense, as a mythology whose archaic effects are no longer with us", in Kaul's words.

Lizeka Mda and Christine Qunta have argued convincingly that reconciliation and the rainbow motif work together to silence dissenting voices, which seek to name racism, by trivialising and appropriating the language of anti-racism necessary for the creation of a just society. Refusal to be complicit in the pervasive denial of difference and the continued effects of history leads to counter-accusations of racism as evidenced in the poster mentioned earlier.

Any mention of race and gender as determinants of position and treatment within the organisation provokes hostility among certain members of the university community. The necessary restructuring is seen as threatening to staff members, even though the Employment Equity Act cannot be to the detriment of, for example, women academics at the University of the Free State, who, at the time, were predominantly congregated at junior lecturer level (70 out of 90) a staggering 72.9 per cent of all women academics at the university. Furthermore, out of 141 full professors at the university, only six were women; 17 out of 73 associate professors were women; 43 out of 165 senior lecturers were women and out of a total of 253 lecturers, 135 were women.

Respondents from the surveys conducted on race and gender by the Faculty of Humanities Equity Committee revealed that staff members experienced numerous employment barriers. There were more disturbing reports that emanated from the student community as well, which suggested that race and gender-motivated violence was not unheard of. There were periods of open race conflict in 1997. My students also made me aware that Black female students who were seen as ambiguous in terms of their sexual orientation had also been threatened. One such woman, seen as a lesbian and threatened with rape in order to "fix" her, was eventually raped by one of the men who threatened her. I was informed of similar threats to other bisexual and lesbian students on campus. Occasions such as these, as well as others too numerous to list here, invite the question, asked by Pumla Gobodo-Madikizela, "[w]hat kind of uhuru is it if the exercise of the right to stand up means that we are exposing ourselves to potential abuse?"

Working in such an environment has had several implications for my teaching activities. Ply D Khusi identifies a relationship between institutional culture and what she calls "the hidden curriculum". This hidden curriculum serves to undermine the reconceptualisation of the systems of knowledge production, as well as meaningful engagement with the discourses of Africa and participation in the reformulation of how Africa registers in the world. Unpacking this hidden curriculum and its relationship to dominant systems of power links with the small numbers and lack of structural power for Black/women staff members at South African universities. Once the hidden curriculum is open to intellectual scrutiny, Khusi suggests, the lessons gleaned from this process can enrich the processes of tertiary education transformation more meaningfully. An interrogation of these dynamics of institutional practice poses further questions about the mode of knowledge production within the more formal educative processes of universities.

Several Black scholars, Kwadi, hooks, Philips and McCaskill among them, have questioned the manner in which knowledge is produced. It becomes clearer that there is an urgent need for epistemologies which "recognize the experiences of black people can be 'scientifically' validated, whatever that means", as hooks asserts. There is an accompanying need to unsettle the belief that knowledge flows unidirectionally from the academe to the community since institutional politics effects the dynamics of the teaching situation. Ketu H Katrak's invitation to post-colonial scholars to "respond to the many urgent needs of their society" is particularly apt here.

Thus far, I have demonstrated the manner in which universities are unable to function as uncontaminated spaces. I have also suggested that we must engage with the networks of dominance and make visible their accompanying systems of violence in order to demolish them. What follows is an examination of how the conservative politics of the university permeate one of the two tiers (research and teaching) seen to contribute to the "central business" of the university: the lecture hall or tutorial room dynamics.

the politics of teaching

Informed by Paulo Freire's substantial and revolutionary corpus, educators have for decades been questioning their own teaching and practice. This has encouraged educators to construct various models of enabling pedagogies suited to the specific areas in which they teach. Inspired by Freire many rejected the traditional archetype of the teacher as all-knowing posited against students as blank slates to be inscribed by their knowledge. Freire's process of conscientisation promised more progressive results. Robin Powers suggests that the servant-leadership is an example of anti-racist and feminist epistemology. For Powers: "[T]he basic tenets of this model state that one is a servant first and leads second. The skills necessary to do this include: listening and understanding; acceptance and empathy; knowing the unknowable beyond conscious rationality; foresight; awareness and perception; and a sense of community and other things."

Ideally, I would find no problem with Powers' argument. Indeed, like bell hooks, I too see the classroom as a location of possibility. However, my experience of teaching at the University of the Free State called into question not only my own assumptions about what models are appropriate in teaching, but also the extent to which I was able to use the tools which I had been able to employ successfully elsewhere. Traditional models value the teacher as omnipotent and it is precisely a deconstruction of this position that allows us as teachers, according to more progressive models, to introduce non-hierarchical dynamics into the teaching situation.

Grappling with the competing discourses on classroom practice gives rise to the question: what are the implications for how our "enabling acts" are read by the students in our classrooms? When I, as a Black woman lecturer, walk into a classroom composed mainly of white male students who are not much younger than I am, what meanings stem from my use of servant-leadership models of teaching? When these students are part of the university I have described and analysed in the preceding sections, this question takes on a particular urgency. And, if indeed, "[t]eaching is a performative act [...] meant to serve as a catalyst that calls everyone to become more and more engaged, to become active participants in learning", as hooks suggests, what participation am I enabling?

What lies beyond the usual theories on paying more attention to disadvantaged students or students from the designated groups? Enabling teaching can be non-hierarchical, we are told. However,

> [t]here are, of course, hierarchies in teaching. Feminists have argued that teaching should be grounded in equality, non-

hierarchy and democracy, but we find this problematic. Whilst a critical pedagogue will not establish him/herself as the definitive source of knowledge about the world, even feminist teachers have knowledge, power and responsibility in the classroom.

The non-hierarchical classroom model was contradictory and counterproductive in my situation at the University of the Free State. The more vocal students at the university in the main regarded any call to independent thinking, taking initiative and so forth, as evidence that the lecturer was ill-prepared. This is a frustration I have often heard articulated by colleagues who do not subscribe to the spoon-feeding model. The quandary here in simple terms is this: if my performance in front of a class made up of the demographic outlined above is one of servant-leadership, I have no faith that it will yield the desired results.

In addition to this, it is misleading to imagine that classrooms can ever be truly non-hierarchical, for learners are not educators within the context of the classroom. When I, then a young, Black academic in my mid-twenties, walked into a first-year lecture at the beginning of the year, there was no instant recognition that I might be the lecturer until I signalled this in some way. I was read as ambiguously located enough in age to possibly be another student. Additionally, the dominant image of the "expert" on any subject is white, male, older. Being Black, female and younger had three discernible simultaneous effects: it challenged the dominant perception of the expert by inviting thinking and the questioning of stereotypes in my students, it marked me as an exceptional Black person/woman/young woman (even though all my friends who were my age had been professionals for several years) and it also ushered in doubts about my ability (maybe less now than when I first arrived there, at the age of 24, in January 1997), since by their own admission, I was one of the first Blackwomen they had encountered in any role outside of (potential) servitude to them.

Servant-leadership then does not challenge their thinking in any way if their expectation is that, as a Blackwoman, servitude is my role or natural station. Forms of servitude can be read as submission, especially when they are seen as natural. It is therefore to be expected that students who respond to me as though I should mother them would do so even more were I to emulate the servant-leadership role. I would not be challenging any preconceived ideas, whether conscious or not. I would simply be confirming patriarchal and racist ideas about what appropriate behaviour is for a person who looks like me.

I prefer to hold on to some aspect of the hierarchy, especially in a context where undermining activity stems equally from students and colleagues. The understanding that the classroom is a space inscribed by the kinds of negotiations propounded by Spivak earlier fuels this. Here I am also positioned in a manner that challenges the status quo given that as Spivak says "I am in the position of power and their teacher and, on the other hand, I am not a bourgeois white male".

When my female students, especially my Black women students, see me as a Blackwoman in a position of power who gives it away by being complicit in my own silencing, they are not empowered. When my white female students see me as unassertive, they are not empowered as women and forced to think about their own possible racism. When my Black male students read me as accommodating, it neither empowers them as oppressed subjects of racism nor challenges their own sexism. If my teaching evokes a reaction in some of my white male and female right-wing students, because it symbolises a threat to all they hold dear, I measure that as some kind of success. So, while my models encourage students to evaluate their own thinking, I remain assertive nonetheless.

There have been successes in this model for me. Student responses to texts that question sexuality, sexual orientation and gender, and how these are permeated by race and class, have been exciting. The matter of hierarchy is one I continue to grapple with, perhaps because I am unable to conceive of what a class without a teacher would look like. I am also convinced that when I stand, Blackwoman, teaching literature and theories by postcolonial Others, the position I hold is *not* the same as if I were teaching the canon in an English Department, in a manner that makes me/my texts invisible, valueless and unvalued. Perhaps given the low status of women (regardless of race), people of colour (regardless of gender and class), gay, lesbian and bi-sexual and non-Christian perspectives, my position in the hierarchy is one of the few ways I have of ensuring that these experiences "will count as knowledge". It makes sense to view this position in Amina Mama's conceptualisation, as one which works to "argue that being implicated in the relations of power does not preclude subversion or engaging in acts that push beyond a given order of things". My use of it here, as part of how I experience universities in South Africa and the ways in which my experience should be opened up for analysis and scrutinised for the lessons it can offer for my teaching and negotiation of this space, is in line with Spivak's observation: "I cannot get a hold of what is meant by a direct pragmatic usefulness which might be unrelated to the classroom".

Universities and how we participate in them as growing numbers of Black people enter them need to receive closer scrutiny. This chapter has participated in what I hope will be an increasing engagement with and into this terrain by what bell hooks calls insurgent intellectuals. Universities are not free from the anxieties that accompany changes in history, the onset of a democratic order and taking pride in one of the most progressive Constitutions ever written. Universities – and institutions in the new South Africa generally – need to be opened up to scrutiny as we analyse and respond to the ways in which configurations of power mutate. The silence around how these structures work, especially from those of us who have an insider/outsider view of their machinations, contributes directly to the mystery which surrounds universities and avoids historicising Blackness in ways that are responsive to historical change. As we continue to challenge, contribute and negotiate within our positions in South African academia, as "black intellectuals [we] must proceed with the understanding that we are not condemned to the margins", hooks reminds us. As members of a national majority with political power, as women or Black people (generally), or Blackwomen (specifically), marginality need not be a position we impose on ourselves. And even if we recognise that margins offer dynamic activism at times, we must be wary of occupying margins in a manner that ghettoises our voices in ways which are anything but subversive, or, in the lingo of kwaito-and-*Yizo-Yizo* urban Black contemporary transgression, ghetto-fabulous.

CHAPTER 8

A mothering feminist's life

A celebration, meditation and roll call

During a panel with four feminist writers, moderator Mohale Mashigo, Yewande Omotoso and Nnedi Okorafor, at the 2016 Open Book Festival in Cape Town, Kabura Nganga asked "how do you/we cultivate feminist joy?"

I answered that we do so through cultivating feminist community, but I felt the inadequacy of my answer. This essay is another meditation on Kabura's invitation.

attention

One day, she called to check on me as she often did, while I had just returned from maternity leave and she found me on the brink of tears from exhaustion and exasperation. I was still learning how to bring the different parts of me together with the most recent transformation, and work was proving particularly difficult. I did not regret choosing to be a mother. I had made the decision with my eyes wide open and adored the baby I held to my breast as I spoke to Elaine on the phone. Not only had I chosen to be a mother consciously, this time, where I had known myself incapable, another time, but I had decided that I would try my best to be the best parent I could be: self-reflexive, attentive, and with a full life of my own.

One of the greatest gifts my parents gave me was this insistence on having their own lives even as they never let me doubt for a minute how essential I was to them, how adored and treasured I was. At thirty-four, I also knew that parenting was a landmine. As much gratitude as I had for how I was raised, at different times in my life I had resented my parents for choices they had made without which I would not have the life they gave me. I knew that this was not something I would be perfect at, that every decision made with love and even the best of intentions could nonetheless erupt into a volcano of arguments between my children and me.

This is what I held in my heart and head as I cried into the phone, but none of this had led to my tears. The source of my exasperation lay elsewhere. I told her about the unreasonable expectations at work that I would be able to do the same amount of work at home that I had done before I had a baby, and my feelings of betrayal because my partner had failed to officially take paternity leave. Although he alternated nights with me, doing night feeds and staying up with our baby so I could sleep, he had suddenly taken to mentioning taking paternity leave later as though it was some writing time. I felt betrayed because we both did work on gender that sought to transform the world, and so, even as he acted out this politics in our home with our baby, I was upset that he had chosen not to make that political step at work. I had known of men colleagues who routinely ridiculed the idea of paternity leave. It cut so deep that my partner had not taken paternity leave, that this decision became the second step in my eventual decision to leave him: the second betrayal we would never be able to come back from.

Elaine listened, as we tried to make sense of what it all meant. We spoke of recognition and the way in which child-rearing is where it can all fall apart even in relationships between people who have lived with feminist principles so long they have become second nature. We had long talked about the ways in which the academy is hostile to women. Indeed, some of our intellectual work directly fought this. And so, she, who knew what it was to pride herself in her work in the academy, and to constantly negotiate the difficulty of being a Blackwoman in the South African academy, was able to hold these different parts of me in conversation. She knew how to listen so that the appropriate analysis could be inserted and magnified in one place, or when it was time for a scandalous joke that made me scream so hard in laughter I startled and woke my sleeping baby, and when to just rage with me. She also knew when to rein me in as I slid kilometres down that slippery slope.

I was telling her about standing in front of a large class, self-conscious of the breast milk I had spilt on my shirt after expressing in my office earlier, as my breasts started to swell up like balloons again, threatening to leak right there as I introduced John Berger's *Ways of Seeing* to my Visual Culture first years. I had rushed from a previous two-hour lecture and did not have time to express again. *When this stupid system was designed, they were not thinking breastfeeding professors could be a thing*, I ranted.

Making sure she was not interrupting, she yanked me off that slope. *Sometimes when I am in Faculty or committee meetings, some of the shit that gets said makes me so mad I wish I had breast milk. It would be messy and they would be horrified, but I would certainly be much happier if I could just whip out a milky breast and just spray them with it. It would also make the point more effectively than the arguments we have to make again and again against the racist patriarchy.*

This was only part joke. Elaine understood deeply the complicated relationships our bodies brought up as women, as Blackwomen, as African feminists. She was in remission from the cancer that would return, a cancer I told her I believed was not just genetic. Work is making you sick, Elaine. I meant her workplace was making her sick. She understood what I meant, and later as my workplace and the incessant demands that I take on more, and more and more made me sick in a different way, she reminded me that the places we work can make us sick. We talked often of ways to replenish our spirits so that we can be healthier for longer.

We spent a few minutes on the breast-milk-in-university-meetings fantasy, and I still chuckle to myself when I think of the craziness and the sheer joy of it as a possibility. On a later date, I did chase my pre-teen nephews around my mother's house shooting white liquid from my nipple when they were irritating me once. It gave me untold pleasure to move my irritation to laughter and their horror. My mother's delighted laughter rang through the house as I did so. I imagine it would be even more rewarding to spray colleagues when they mouth offensive diatribe parading as civilised critique.

On Elaine's last visit home, I did not realise it was her goodbye trip as we sat at a restaurant in Pretoria, half teasing her daughter, Jessica, about how I had changed her nappy once, marvelling at Miles, her son, now a young man, and talking about how good she looked. I knew the cancer was back. I did not want to know that she would not kick it into remission again.

As I read her cancer diaries, I rooted for her, and refused the flickering recognition that she was leaving. I have lost so many loved ones to cancer that I had to pretend really hard that what I was seeing meant something else. Her beautiful body had transported her across desert and sea, across hurt and forgiveness, and now, her generous, dangerous body had turned on her. But she wrote and made sense of it until the end.

Elaine taught me how to hold the strange bits of me together as though this was my design. Conversation slipped easily between parenting to sex to frivolity to high theory. With Elaine, feminism was sisterhood, brilliance, courage and laughter. It was also the place where our grown up selves and our little girl selves kissed and cavorted.

play

She wrote an essay on the difficulties and embattlement of being a feminist who had conceded to the lobola process. She participated and thought her way through it. It had been harder than she had anticipated, and I was amazed that she owned up to it, even though feminists are renowned for our big mouths, our disrespect for norms and conventional wisdom. I understood that there were feminists who liked to pretend it was easy to fight with your family all the time. Lobola was a topic that had come up regularly in conversation with my friends from the time we entered an age, in our twenties, where marriage was something to consider. Some friends had simply gone through with it, with differing levels of patience and discomfort. Some had fought it again and again, sometimes winning and other times losing. When I read Danai's piece, I was dazed. I read it again and again, marvelling at her candour. I knew these would be a source of harsh judgement, that some would find her feminism wanting as a result. I did not. I tried to imagine what it must feel like to be inside a marriage while constantly reflecting on the demands of performing all of these things that buy you space to build a different kind of life with your love. I found her honesty breath-taking.

I had read several pieces by her when I met her for the first time, a meeting to which she brought her baby. I realised she had driven across town in the heat, had parked at the furthest possible point because not only was parking a scarcity, but this outpost was reserved for graduate students. She had then manoeuvred herself up a hill, heavy laptop on shoulder, bouncing baby in a pram around pathways that were not designed for all she needed to bring. She spoke with absolute clarity as if she had not just climbed a hill and I marvelled at how calm she was, how collected her thoughts and how determined she was to get through the project we discussed – three anomalies in the academy who would not apologise for our presence.

Two of us in that room – a man and a woman – dedicated to feminist parenting tried to play with her baby, used as we were to parenting while working, as a way to signal something like care to her. It was not that she needed it, but more perhaps that we needed to give this unspoken signal of our care and recognition.

Later, as our friendship grew stronger until she was my sister, I watched her effortlessly juggle multiple arts with a level of expertise that I am still dazzled watching. I did not know you could be a feminist genius of the academy who cooks meals that belong in designer cookbooks, knows how to decorate like a designer and write poetry like a sage. And sometimes, because my friend will fight an injustice so hard and speak up for any maligned and brutalised, I sometimes have to hold her back to remind her that she needs to leave some energy for herself.

And with her, I have sometimes marathon-laughed so hard that we both collapsed from exhaustion. We have shared shock and disappointment at the limits of heterosexual co-parenting, and managed our upset children's voices on the other side of the phone as we sat in international airports on different continents. And I always admire that candour that struck me in my first encounter with her work. She is never without her truthfulness and integrity, even when I do not want to know what is wrong with what I have just done. It is a friendship that knows when the moment requires loyalty and when appraisal is required.

She is also one of my child's many safe places. I watch as our children – who long ago, with no prompting from us adopted each other as siblings – grow deeper into a love relationship with each other. I love eavesdropping with her as they finish each other's sentences and have the kinds of strange conversations that small children seem too young for. My squeamishness is a long running joke among many of my friends, whereas Danai has such an advanced and integrated sense of self that she is almost impossible to gross out. The two of them are the only children who, having each once vomited all over me, made me worry rather than sending me on my own squeamish fit.

Danai teaches me that feminism demands that we live with an open heart, and that the rewards of feminist choice are infinite: as serious as defying secrecy and as joyful as jumping into puddles.

breath

As I sat in my gynaecologist and obstetrician's reception area, I could not have been more physically uncomfortable. It was my final check up in a pregnancy that had gone very well but for my high weight gain brought about mainly by my out of character desire for endless carbohydrates. They call it cravings. Pregnancy at thirty-four was immersion in renegotiating relationships with my body. It was sometimes like an introduction to the workings of a body unlike mine, as to be expected. There are many humorous tales on trying to move in a way I had learnt to take for granted over three or two decades only to realise my body could not oblige. As my partner sat next to me chatting away as we waited for our appointment, and the friendly receptionist announced that my appointment would be cancelled since another patient had gone into labour, I was not sure how to feel. The appointment was routine, but I would have liked the assurance that we were on track.

When Caroline, Achieng's birth partner, and a mutual friend came out to announce that it was Achieng who had gone into labour, I remember feeling slightly alarmed for her and happy she had taken my slot.

Years later I never tire of reminding her of her timing. *You decided to go into labour at the very hour I was supposed to see Dr Malepule Mseleku for the last time before my own labour.* Achieng's sense of time is meticulous, so I like to joke that she had timed this deliberately too.

Our sons, born exactly four weeks apart, at the hands of the same obstetrics whizz, played together before they could construct sentences. And as we watched them grow, we slowly and carefully built a friendship of our own. We have been growing into mothering together from the very beginning, tentatively, playfully, reassuring each other and admitting senses of inadequacy that do not come easily to us highly accomplished professionals with PhDs who knew, before parenting, how to pack up our lives to live in countries whose languages we did not speak prior to arrival.

Sometimes, I call her up with a minor crisis almost in tears from rage or dramatic pain, and she can tell whether to take it seriously or to just laugh at me until I am laughing at myself with her.

It does not occur to her to hold back how many times her son tells her she is not such fun and he wishes I had birthed him. I know he does not mean it no matter how many times he says it. He adores his mother. It does not occur to her to mind that he fantasises about another mother. Not only does she laugh it off, she changes from telling him to deal with his tough luck to giving him permission to move to my house. And although she feared it, she let me take our sons across the country on a beach holiday she was not invited to. My heart melted as she admitted that she could not imagine letting anyone else take him away in this way.

On my longest trip away from home since my son was born, she picks him up for days at a time. He tells me he only sort of misses me. I know it has everything to do with how she takes care of him; that she knows his every facial expression, every eccentricity. I know that nine years later our sons' play dates are unpredictable. Sometimes, they need a little distance from each other. At other times, it is as if they cannot breathe enough of each other's air.

When I thank her again and again, she brushes it off, as if two strong-willed children are the easiest thing in the world to manage. And I remember the look of recognition on her face as I told her I was leaving him to take up a visiting professorship on another continent for a month. As single parents, every decision is tempered with what effect this will have on your child. I have seen her squeeze several continents into a seven-day trip, determined to do her work, but also mindful of the needs of a small child – hers. She has seen me arrive, jetlagged from a trip via two continents with annoying layovers, only to realise that I was required to cheer on the side-lines at my son's athletics day.

As feminists raising boys, we are determined to live our lives in ways that make the most sense. They need to grow up knowing the value of a full life for all genders, to take it as norm, to understand that love and work are human endeavours that are chosen and negotiated every day. Mothering is a site of contradictions, and neither one of us is interested in being superwoman. However, the lines between responsible parenting and the self-sacrifice that our dominant culture expects from women, on the one hand, and the one between belonging to yourself and harming your child through inattentiveness, on the other, are sometimes marked on sandy not rocky shores. Each wave blurs them further.

This is a friendship that brings untold joy, in which no conversation subject is taboo, not even the most embarrassing attempts at finding love, the strangest betrayals or most outrageous workplace violence. Sometimes when I hear people describe the personality of the late great Maya Angelou: her fierceness, her absolute refusal to be associated with anything she could not claim in the bright light of day, this unshakeable commitment to belong to herself, her grace and generosity, it is Achieng I hear them describe. Achieng is not just another mother to my child, and friend to every part of my spirit. Achieng teaches me that feminism is about knowing when to let go and when to receive.

heart

I remember the day we started becoming friends, a few weeks after our twenty-first birthdays, although I could never have predicted how indispensable his friendship would become to me and remain more than two decades later. He is my son's favourite uncle, which is funny, considering how he felt about children once.

In our twenties, when I was not going to have children and he shared the same choice, we would often list reasons why our lives would be better off without parenting. He did not quite like children, he would say, although he does take them seriously when they are around. I quite like children, I would add, I just don't particularly want them to stay and mess all my things up. I am much too selfish in my taste and wanderlust to make the adjustments necessary to accommodate children. One does not birth children unless you can raise them properly. Well, people do this all the time, but we are not those people.

Some of our friends found our choices to opt out of parenting strange given how close we both were to our respective parents. It was with slight trepidation that I made a phone call across the country to tell him I was pregnant. I knew that friendships changed when children were introduced, and that some friends failed to find each other again. This was not a friendship I wanted to ever live without. When another of his closest friends also announced her pregnancy, she and I decided to worry together.

But nothing anyone imagined could have prepared Thoko or I for the centrality of Angelo to our children's lives. His generosity to them knows no bounds, and they understand his rules. My son is often taken aback when we remind him that we were friends before he was even an idea.

He knew me so well that when he called me one day from his new job in Pietermaritzburg, he could tell I was overwhelmed. My partner and I had agreed that he needed time to finish a multi-year project whose ending had been postponed, and that to do so he needed the physical distance. I imagined I could cope. But, as the project's end proved elusive and his return again postponed, I regretted that decision. More than this, I resented the repeated absences that rendered me a single parent when I had consciously decided against just such a position.

And so, as Angelo called, I mentioned some of this as we discussed family, work, laughed, critiqued and teased each other as we had been doing for half our lives. He teased me about being an old woman, a recurrent joke, since he was born exactly three weeks after me. He was gentle in commenting on my fatigue, and angry at my parenting alone.

That weekend, and several times that year, he flew to Johannesburg for weekends during which I was so happy to see him I cried. He was furious with my then partner who had chosen just then to flail when faced with parenting our baby, and loving to me, his friend, whom he had never seen so out of sorts, and whisperer to my son who thinks he can do no wrong. I imagined myself in a relationship with a man who valued the feminist principles and values we both claimed. But here was a reality that increasingly led to a series of betrayals of who we had said we were. To be clear, I do not think the betrayal was only to me. It was a betrayal to what we had said we would build in a life together, the third one our partnership would never recover from.

My friend stepped into this, in the very spirit of who *he* had always been. Given the size of academic salaries, his visits to coparent with me were as emotionally noble as they were materially generous. To negotiate the morass that is South African academia for a Black person all week, and then choose not rest for the weekend, but to fly across the country to be at the side of someone he loves is not something we are all capable of. The difference it made, and the meaning it holds for me makes me cry to this day.

He has an unmatched ability to treat both my son and me as though we each are his primary interest even as we all sit in the same room. He does not always tell me what I want to hear, but he is always on my side. Nearly a decade later, I watch how our children cannot imagine life without him.

Over more than half our lives now, Angelo teaches me that feminism is not just talk, and the stuff of our academic research and the engine of our creative writing. He teaches me that feminism is love and work every day, that sometimes, feminist love's beauty and life-changing power is so profound that it still makes me weep nearly a decade later.

moon

She is the only person I have ever stalked into friendship. As I lay on my bed reading one of the many publications I read each month in those days, turning the pages of a very popular Black women's magazine, I read a short interview with her about her work in a feminist technology organisation. The work itself sounded fascinating, and this long before I would think about the gendering of technology. She also spoke quite candidly about being a feminist in the world and a desire this identity produced that she was struggling to meet.

She craved a community of Black feminists in South Africa. In later years, it seemed typically her to declare this desire in a magazine that, like many women's magazines, has such a conflicted relationship with feminism. Never one to temper herself or mute her voice, this was a space as good as any.

When I read this interview in my sixteenth-floor Westdene, Bloemfontein flat, I belonged to such a community. It was a mobile community of Black feminists mostly in academia, publishing and the heritage industry that we had formed, transformed and nurtured. Started through specific meetings in a room to address various levels of invisibilisation as Blackwomen in the academy, as we grew and moved, it had now taken on a virtual presence as well.

Having read the interview over the weekend, I resolved to reach out to her. And so it was that the following Monday, before I went to class, I sent off an email to her inviting her to join my community. A few months later, I was delighted to see we were on the same programme for the same feminist workshop in the Western Cape. It was a fantastic workshop and the beginning of a beautiful, transformative friendship.

It is a friendship that does what all of the best kinds of friendship achieve. It requires work and is forgiving of the times when we do not put in the work the friendship deserves. We were young women brimming with confidence, taking, as she likes to say "like ducks to water" to a world and country rapidly changing. We were brave in the face of challenges and opportunities that would have been unimaginable in the country we grew up in as Blackgirls, a country that was morphing dramatically into something we could not yet fully grasp.

As we transformed our lives, and ourselves, we have also had to grapple with who we were when faced with ageing parents. A curious inversion happens when parents' fragility starts to temper their previous full autonomous and independent lives. We are both very much our parents' daughters in personality, in eccentricity and in political inclination.

Another friend, older by a decade, once confessed to the

enormous guilt she feels at how much she resents her parents for getting old. We sat and tried to make sense of it, none of us fully grasping it. I realise now that some of the resentment comes from being faced with our own future maturing and our parents' mortality.

And so, when first I, then she, lost a parent each to cancer, it made us re-examine everything we had ever taken for granted about ourselves, family and decisions to parent. The death of a beloved parent with whom you have had a lifelong close relationship changes you forever. It is as if we were learning to walk again. And to hold as part of that mourning the inability of the surviving parent to cope with that loss is dizzying. But we continue to learn to walk anew, accepting, for instance, that my father and Gail's mother will never hold our son.

In the many years of our friendship, we have road-tripped, and have literally driven through a cloud together. I have called her in the middle of the night and cried "please come get me", and she has rocked up with her Harvard tracksuit over her pyjamas a few minutes later and scooped me up.

Sometimes she has nurtured me, and other times she has lectured me. And she never believes any of my romantic relationship plans. When thrice I decided – and then decided against – marriage, she confessed to having looked at the prospective spouses and stopped short of saying out loud "poor sod, you really believe this will happen". It is very frustrating that she is always right about these plans. But friendship sometimes means you know people better than they know themselves. She understands my ambivalence at a deeper level than I can grasp.

As if all of this is not enough, once a week for the better part of a decade, she picks our son up in the afternoon, plays with, feeds and mothers him, tucks him in, lets him run into her bed when he has nightmares. And, having fed and watered him, she drops him off at school in the morning.

When she moved to a new house, which she extensively renovated, my son came home elated from discussing plans for his new room and bathroom there. She has created such substantial room for him in her life that it makes sense that he speaks of her as his second mother. And, even when she is really *naar* with me, her commitment to him is unwavering. For a single mother, the gift of time is rarest, most treasured of all.

I have seen the strain on the faces and hearts of single parent friends who do not have this reprieve and know without a doubt that without it, I could not be the parent I am for the six other nights and mornings. Gail teaches me that feminism is principled, generous and non-negotiable. She teaches me that feminist friendship is unsurpassed.

north

She dislikes talking on the phone. Do you know how strange it is to be an opinionated, loud-mouthed feminist who is a delight in conversation but who does not like talking on the phone?

But so what if it is strange?

We met through Gail many years ago on one of my trips from Bloemfontein to Johannesburg during which I partly stayed with Gail. I could see why they were close, how they finished each other's sentences, and relished in the loving beauty of a friendship between women who did not even think to compete with each other.

A few years later, after I had moved to Gauteng, I arrived at her house with another friend, Pumeza, to meet Xoliswa's new baby. And, I will never forget what Xoliswa said, as I held her baby, because it freed me more than anything I have ever heard said about mothering.

> *My baby has a life, and will have a bigger life. I have a life. We are building our life together. She is not my life and I am not hers. I have a great life that I have worked quite hard to design just as it is. I have no intention of giving it up. It's a relationship of love and nurturing and guidance and responsibility and yes, there will be sacrifice, as there should be. But I will not sacrifice myself to*

motherhood. It would be a horrible thing to do to myself, and an injustice to my child.

And, as I listened to her, I realised for the first time why mothering had been a choice I had opted out of. I adore my mother who has always had her own professional life, so that I could take that for granted. Part of the memory of being her child has also been her insistence that as her children, we were her whole life. Sometimes it would be expressed as the declaration that she lives for her children. I remember as a fiercely independent child, and young woman, how confusing this sentiment was to me.

I learnt that mothering done well requires living for your children, and I did not understand what that meant. Now I recognise that it means the same thing I mean when I tell my children that they are my heart. However, because my mother's words were not spoken in a vacuum, but into a world that socialises us to think about mothering as the culmination of a woman's achievement, I could not imagine that mothering could feel free.

As I listened to Xoliswa then, with her baby there, seeing that this desire to belong to herself had not been snuffed out by childbirth was a delight to behold. She was the same person. It was possible to belong to yourself and be committed to parenting well. She felt certain that she would never sacrifice herself. I had always known that I would be incapable of self-sacrificing and still parenting well. And in a few sentences, she had freed me.

She has freed me many times over the years. There have been times when I have arrived at her house for a few hours with my child and we both end up leaving two days later. I have never seen a film of hers I was not blown away by, not just because of how she returns to women's and girls' lives, but also the choices she makes aesthetically and ideologically about how to represent them. In her films, her subjects always have interpretative authority.

Recently I was informed by the woman who takes care of my child, who has been my employee since my son was two months old, that for many years and without my knowledge, Xoliswa calls when I am on a trip to check if they need anything. She calls to make sure my son wants for nothing. And, on the trip I almost did not take because I was not sure my nine-year-old and I could survive a month without each other, she took him for a weekend and kept him for a week. When I talked to him that week, he told me he only sort of missed me.

Xoliswa always tells me the truth, even when it means we will fight. She is startlingly honest about her own mistakes, faults and failures. I have had to teach her to keep a little more of herself for herself because her generosity can also be her biggest weakness. She knows her own mind and unapologetically pursues her dreams, but not at any cost. She truly believes the Universe is generous but she has "no fucking time" for misogynists and other fascists. It would take a year to list all the things she teaches me. And her daughter has the same spirit, so she challenges and stretches us both. Xoliswa is a feminist who belongs to herself, a wonder to love.

And so it is that mothering is something I take enormous pride and pleasure in. It is a decision I am pleased to have made, all the hard work and unpredictability notwithstanding. I would not have made it this far without these feminists who hold my hand, hold my heart, and help me think myself into and out of situations. They save my life by making it possible in its messy, thorny, adventurous and joyful range.

Finally, when I say feminism has saved my life more times than I can imagine, I mean my own, and I mean the love, friendship, brains and community of the feminists in my life too. This is what feminism is.

CHAPTER 9

When I grow up, I want to be me/you

Blackwomen, Joyful Struggle and the Academy

> *And there are black women considered so dangerous*
> *in South Africa they prison them away*
> — GRACE NICHOLS

At the beginning of 2005, I attended a gathering at the University of the Western Cape's Gender Equity Unit in which Mary Hames invited us to reflect on Black women's feminist academic activism. To arrive at this space, to listen and come into contact with women whose work I did not know, or whose work I held in high regard was a rare pleasure. It was a room full of women from different public sector spaces, academia, NGOs and the creative industries. While all of the feminists there gathered cared deeply about the connections between changing the world and knowledge production, we very seldom thought about our own work – collectively and individually – as worthy of analysis and as subject for a conference. But Mary Hames insisted that we bring ourselves – in varied messy, complicated, hopeful, ambivalent energetic ways – to this setting. It was joyful. It was hard work. The hard work was in sitting with the discomfort of knowing we were not sure what we meant when we said "self-care". The hard work was not knowing who we were as thinking, loving, determined, bleeding, dancing Blackwomen who answered to feminist when we did not have to defend ourselves for three whole days. Every one of us believed in safe spaces, closed spaces and knew that feminism saved our lives several times over. But we did not know what feminist safety and home felt like, and here we all were, determined to create it, live it, breathe it in and surrender to it.

Many of us were engaged in work against erasure: much of our work was archival in one way or another. Deirdre Prins was trying to figure out how to create a visual and conceptual language that captured time for Africans in her poetry, while trying to imagine a museum practice that inspired and respected memory without memorials and recourse to the spectacular modes of representation that had become so beloved of her profession by day. Yvette Abrahams was trying to figure out how to keep writing about ancestors who come to us through colonial record and through other transmissions of knowledge we are not trained to harness. Sometimes we had to pioneer not just fields of work but also strategies of survival. Accepting Mary Hames' invitation, we had to reflect on pleasure, on what it means to think about feminist legacies beyond claiming them.

What does an anti-racist feminist presence look like? Beyond saying "there have always been feminists in Africa, we are not anomalies", what did that story of feminist presence look like in our minds, on our bodies, in our hearts? How did we mark it in our essays, short stories, our films, exhibitions and workshops? What does it mean to bring academic and activist into coalition, collision and dance? What would a collective feminist stock-taking look like for the Blackwomen gathered in that room?

I start this chapter with an excerpt from a poet whose words I have turned and returned to since a first accidental encounter at a bookshop that no longer exists on Rondebosch Main Road. It is no accident that seeing the title *i is a long memoried woman* immediately grabbed my twenty-one-year-old eye. My friend, Angelo and I were on one of our many book-shopping trips, and were actually headed to a second-hand bookshop in Claremont in which we regularly found previously banned, out of print, and "obscure" Black writing, but we had stopped at this bookshop because we were in search of a hard-to-find book that had earned its writer a fatwa. The dangerous book was unoffocially on sale at the detour bookshop, and we were determined to get our copies. We left with copies of *Satanic Verses* and began a long love affair with Grace Nichols on the page. Beginning this chapter with Grace Nichols' words from a later collection of poems seems apt: the echo of memory, the transnational connections, the imaginative power, the embrace of the counter-intuitive. All of these were part of the work we tried to do at that conference.

Hames' was a gathering of dangerous women, some of them directly the women Nichols speaks about in the lines above – women who had been detained, stoned, shot at, hounded, banned – and many of us simply inheritors of their audacity. This essay, which is a much revised version of the thoughts I presented as offering, is part engagement with Hames' invitation.

It is important to acknowledge the energies that went into *realising* that gathering in all the meanings conjured up by that word: thought it up, stumbled upon it, recognised it, and made it a reality. It is not often that so many of us who answer to "African feminist" and/or "Black feminist" to "womanist" are able to gather under one roof for a few days and think and learn from each other. Obviously this has less to do with our will or desire for such occasions than with the many other things we are busy doing as we stubbornly insist on working towards more interestingly creative, increasingly humane and unashamedly revolutionary existences in our work and lives, for we all know that the onslaught from homophobic, white supremacist capitalist patriarchy is relentless.

Since then, I can still count the number of times I sat in a hall, and knew the bodies that peopled it were like me in their opposition to homophobia, racism, patriarchy and capitalism. Having been to numerous Black Studies, African Studies, Postcolonial Studies, and Feminist conferences of different kinds is not the same thing.

How delicious was it to sit there secure in the knowledge that I needed not be nervous when someone offers to crack a joke in such a setting? Humour has historically been such a double-edged sword for people of the African world.

I asked my sisters there gathered: When was the last time you could even entertain this community, physically manifested, as a possibility? Perhaps it was in your activist days, trying to topple the apartheid regime and you assumed that most of your comrades shared in your version of revolutionary zeal. For many of the younger ones, this may be a first or second.

All of these years later, I remain grateful to Mary Hames, Vanessa Ludwig, Nontle Baji and all the other people at the Gender Equity Unit who made this gathering a reality. I remain grateful to the energies of the Blackwomen who had established the Gender Equity Unit at UWC alongside and under the leadership of Rhoda Kadalie. It does not matter how much I battle with her writing these days, or how strongly I have disagreed with an argument she has vigorously defended. Part of the feminist work of reflecting on the long trajectories and many circuits of Black women's work demands a recognition of what her work enabled and continues to enable. Institutions are hard to build, and feminist institutions are under constant attack. The story of feminist thinking is not just about acknowledging how we benefit from those we still agree with, share with. It is much harder.

Myesha Jenkins says that this feeling of recognition, a feeling that I insist on calling homing, is our 'birthright', in her poem of the same name:

I am
because of women

I come
from women
I know
because of women
I pray
to the spirits of women
I fight
for women
I am inspired
by women
I stand
with women
I am loved
by women
I too
love women

I am a woman

That forum offered us all an amazing possibility to reflect without the onslaught, to learn from each other, laugh with and acknowledge our various efforts, to listen to women whose thinking inspires and homes me. It was a rare chance to let our guards down. So, the crafting of such a space where we are reflected in our varied manifestations is a wonderful thing.

I am taking a little bit of time to dwell on this because even though African feminists ingesting these words know what I am saying to be true: the rarity, the excitement, the homing, etc., we don't say it often enough. As much as we get done, as much as we stand up against, as much as we imagine, we do not tell each other enough or own the successes we work so hard for.

It is probably our training as Africans that makes us like this: the African aversion to immodesty that often sees someone die before her praises are sung, our socialisation that work should be for the benefit of the whole, and the like. It is particularly ironic that as feminists who spend so much time owning, claiming and defending the names of the women who came before us, who write them into histories of the world, we spend so little time doing the same to the sisters in our midst who still walk the earth embodied in ways we can see. I think it is quite a puzzling eccentricity that we who teach ourselves continuously – and all the girl children and young women we mother, older-sister, and otherwise encourage – to love the kinks in their hair, to make peace with the regular unpredictabilities of menstrual cycles, and other such, do not pat ourselves on the back enough.

The gathering offered the potential to think about one another's work over a few days, to have the conversations we often wish we could have if we were not so frequently weighed down with distractive, destructive energy-sappers in our everyday work. We all crave conversations where we can start from the same premise, even when we disagree, as we sometimes did over the three days. And the work that went into conceiving and planning this, as well as getting all of us here at the same time, is quite remarkable. Its acknowledgment cannot be the cursory one we are often obliged to give to funders, supervisors, colleagues, and so forth in our intellectual activist work.

The unabashed, uncluttered proximity with which it places "intellectual" and "activism" frees us from defending the necessity of activism in academia, or insisting on the recognition of intellectual energy in the NGO sector. I am flagging those contributions that the conference makes, and I pay attention to words because I am a lover, crafter and student of words.

fifteen-year-old feminist

When I was fifteen, I told a visiting career guidance counsellor that I was a feminist in the first sentence when she asked me to tell her about myself. She frowned, and remarked on how young I was to be feminist. I thought she was being really stupid, but, because I had been raised well, kept this to myself. I had been feminist/womanist since I could remember. But I had just discovered the word "feminist" and was in love with the knowledge that I and others could use it, and in its use we would be able to recognise shared worldviews and ways of living without saying another word. My chancing upon the *word* made me embrace it as a signal of a community of women who questioned.

Seventeen years later, as I mixed, mingled and learnt from the Gender Equity Unit conference, I could look back at my younger self and smile at the memories of how that feminism articulated itself in self-loving and sometimes misguided ways. I knew that my admiration for and emulation of daredevil antics had much to do with defining myself in ways that excited me. I knew that I have always been fascinated by transgressive women and read the defiance that was labelled crazy as evidence of intellect and agency. I was to learn the word "agency" much later.

I was also particularly fascinated by teenage girls, largely because I had spent the first decade of my working life teaching young people about words, beauty and power, and also because my first niece was gradually growing in that direction. My eye is still drawn to the non-conformists among my students: the ones who wear outrageous T-shirts and hats, those who ask unusual questions, and offer thought-through analyses of the minor characters in a novel. It seems to me that there is as much competition for the boundaries of identity now as there were when I was a teenager.

girl power ≠ young feminism

At the same time, in recent years I had grown increasingly conflicted by a phenomenon described as girl power. Initially I was fascinated by it since it suggested a feminist consciousness in its naming. That response was soon complicated by overt celebrations of patriarchally sanctioned performances of womanliness by many girl power proponents: the love of Barbie, all material things pink (but not the disruptive queer politics of pink), with claims of independence. This reminds me of Gayatri Chakravorty Spivak's thinking on how the centre, the hegemony, always survives through stealing from subversive language and practice in order to better fortify itself and offer the pretence that it is less violating than it in actual fact is. Spivak seems to speak directly to the phenomenon of girl power.

I had recently left my employment as a senior lecturer at a public university, to take up a post in a different research environment. At the University of the (Orange) Free State where I taught for ten years, I had been repeatedly struck by the ways in which an overtly political feminist consciousness was less visible among my students than it was when I was at university in the early nineties. My students were not much younger than I when I started teaching there, at 24, but the gap had widened somewhat as I left. Throughout that period I was also often pained by how many clearly objectifying practices were seen as evidence of a feminist consciousness. One of the systems that we discussed as feminist friends and colleagues at my previous institution was the "sugar daddy" syndrome where an older man has an intimate relationship with a much younger woman that he then bestows financial favours on.

I suspect I drove Barbara Mashope, Angie Khumalo, Mariza Brooks and Helene Strauss particularly insane with my obsessive attempts to make sense of the "sugar daddy" phenomena on campus. Fresh in my own mind had been the sometimes predatory interest of older men with professions and German sedans in us as undergraduates when I had been a student in Cape Town. While I was careful not to draw easy connections between my undergrad experiences at UCT and the phenomenon I was witnessing on the campus I taught at, several concerns remained with me.

"Sugar daddies" were not a new phenomenon. The dynamics of the exploitative relationship between much older man and younger, sometimes adolescent woman, have not changed that much. And after all these years I have not figured out whether the older man is thus named because he gets sugar, a euphemism for sexual intercourse, or if he provides sugar, in the form of the pleasure that his money brings. Perhaps this etymology is less important than the discursive vocabulary used to name, justify and describe these relationships.

Popular discourse at UFS labelled these young women as empowered, in control and exhibiting "girl power". These adolescents listen to the Destiny's Child liberal feminist anthem, 'Independent women', at the same time that they dance to lyrics that ask "don't you wish your girlfriend was hot like me?" where women compete for the ultimate prize: the heterosexual man. These young women, in the process of some professional training for future financial independence, seek out "sugar daddies" who give them money in exact contradiction to their anthem that asserts the importance of a woman buying things – a car, a house, clothes, a diamond ring – for herself and not needing a man to take care of her. I battled to locate the space for irony.

Notwithstanding the offered explanations, these "sugar daddy" relationships are very clearly exploitative, and unlike legitimate sex-work in their dishonesty. And many in my generation – and in my students' generation – knew of how dangerous and deadly these relationships often were. We were all familiar with the misogynist language for speaking about undergraduate university women's bodies available for collection over weekends, the automatic access, the euphemism for rape as men in their thirties and forties boasted about sex with fifteen- and sixteen-year-olds. After many years of conversations about the power dynamics of such exchange, I remained unconvinced by the claims that the young women involved are hereby asserting control over their sexuality. Many adolescents insist that this arrangement is transitory, and upon graduation, the "sugar daddy" is made redundant. This was certainly part of the picture. They defended these relationships by pointing to the manner in which they choose what to get in exchange – which designer-label outfits, how much money, which electronic gadget – for their sexual favours and company. They denied a contradiction in claimed status as independent women and the idolising of women celebrity achievers on the one hand, and the decision to enter "sugar daddy" exchanges on the other. The morality of it all was as uninteresting to me then, as it is now. I remain unconvinced about the romanticisation of agency – and the glossing over of violence – in relationships so skewed by power.

I asked the gathering at the UWC Gender Equity Unit to help me through some questions and the limitations of my own thinking. How does the language of feminism, of sexual pleasure and reproductive choice, of the enabling legislation that many feminists put in place in South Africa, get co-opted into what is so classically patriarchal? What kinds of responsibilities does such a situation present for those of us who do answer to feminist? Faced with such puzzling challenges, it might be easy to feel slightly deflated. I think it is also easy to lose sight of some of the gains we have made, and continue to realise. At the same time, I was not entirely pessimistic about what directions girl power suggested for the terrain of women's sexuality.

When I was in high school, women's reproductive choice had to be asserted over and over again, frightening numbers of young women died every year (or were permanently scarred) when they attempted to terminate pregnancies. I do not even want to think about how many of these women were then reported to the police by doctors when they could no longer take the pain, the bleeding, or both and went to GPs, clinics and hospitals for help. When they eventually left the hospital, criminalised, they were thrown out of school. We will never know how many young women sat through the pain and questions, too afraid to go to a gynaecologist until more than a decade later. It was also a time when young women who chose, or felt compelled, to carry their pregnancies to full term were also expelled while the young men who impregnated them were allowed to continue their schooling uninterrupted. It was also a time of the open secret where some predatory male teachers were the fathers of children birthed by girls previously in their classrooms. We very rarely said "child abuse" in public, and now we wonder where this mysterious scourge comes from so suddenly. Then there were high demands on us sexually and a range of ridiculous explanations for what was happening. There were so many deaths from abortions, one of these arguments went, because we were part of the lost generation aimlessly wandering about, and promiscuous; a particularly hurtful accusation for a generation of youth in the apartheid eighties.

Some of us tapped into this memory in the letters of outrage we wrote to two Eastern Cape newspapers, *Daily Dispatch* and *The Eastern Cape Herald* in June 2003 in outrage as a result of Lydia Makwente's rape and murder by young men from her school and township in Mdantsane and asserted:

> It is ironic and deeply painful that although South Africa is now a democracy, girl-children and young women continue to be under attack in their own communities and homes. While there were systems in place which worked to terrorise us as Black girls growing up under apartheid both from the state and from some people in our various communities, there appear to be fewer safe spaces for little girls and young women growing up today.

I now no longer remember which of the newspapers published the letter. Today, we have had collective wins and nowhere more so than at the legislative level, and yet, young Blackwomen are still under siege. We all know that some challenges remain at the level of implementation, but all those right-wing attempts to reverse freedom of choice legislation failed. The girl power generation has a somewhat paradoxical relationship to sexual and reproductive choice. Nonetheless, it remains a wonderful thing that most of them will not die from terminated pregnancies even as they continue to live under threats of rape from a man they know, or "curative rape" if they are lesbian.

We continue to live in dangerous and exciting times. Nor are these contradictions only present at the level of student populations in academia. At staff levels, it is an interesting time to be a Black woman academic in South Africa. The essays in the collection that Reitumetse Obakeng Mabokela and Zine Magubane in 2005 edited testify to this.

Many of us remember a time when we ached for Blackwomen, or just Blackmen lecturers and tutors. One of my biggest gripes was that I had managed to miss both Zoë Wicomb's and Naledi Pandor's brief teaching at University of Cape Town's English Department when I was an undergraduate; that I had not been young enough to have had Desiree Lewis head my classes. In the early to mid-nineties, we often complained about what a difference it would have made to see ourselves more extensively reflected in the world of academic authority. It was in this spirit that my very good friend, Madeleine Jenneker, insisted that we attend every lecture offered by Prof van der Westhuizen, who was a Medievalist, because he was the only Black lecturer we had in the UCT English department when we were undergraduates. It did not matter that we found the world of Medieval England rather frightening and unattractive, and that all that repression made us gag. I was an older postgraduate student studying in England when the more disruptive aspects of Chaucer's work were revealed to me.

As we grew up and some of us chose to teach at universities, part of the challenge we took on was one of setting about making this different. It was not only what we taught that was important, but how, when, and so on. Several of the essays in the Magubane and Mabokela book on the experiences of Blackwomen in South African academia speak to this complicated politics of location in academe. These essays note the challenges of misrecognition: constant suggestions that Blackwomen enter through the back door not merit, the sexual and racial harassment, the stereotyping as safe/soft option as a woman, the usual allegations of hypersensitivity that Black professionals have to deal with everywhere, and so forth. They speak of near court cases, legal battles and myriad other problems. In those chapters edited by Mabokela and Magubane, we also discuss some of the joyful lessons that have come with that process.

The latter include watching young students who come to voice in the classes we offer, the presence of young women, who not only come to feminism, but sometimes just come out due to some things we, as lecturers, might have said in class; the ability to perform older-sistering, which is crucial in academia, lagging behind as it is in terms of overall transformation. This activity that I like to call older-sistering goes by the names "mentoring" and "role-modelling" at other times. My preference for older-sistering is due to the room that name allows both parties to manoeuvre, challenge and focus simultaneously on younger siblings in that environment and your own development. It seems to me that mentoring is often used to refer to younger Black people coming into previously white professional settings, where the incoming professional is to be shown the ropes but does not really offer anything to the aid of the mentor. It seems like a strangely uni-directional and condescending relationship since the mentor is seen to be fully developed in and of herself. Older-sistering does not literally require that the "older sister" be older in calendar years, but only that she be the one who has been in the work situation the longest.

Some of the benefits of our vocal presence in the corridors of academia stem from the pure symbolic power that our presence has for students who have not seen authority embodied by Black feminists before. In my chapter in Mabokela and Magubane's book, I wrote about how when I first arrived at the University of the Free State, I was one of the first Blackwomen some of my white students had seen outside of positions of servitude to them. I was also frequently a surprise for many of my Black students who expected me to look different – older and more masculine – even after they had seen my name. Even as a minority, we often achieved a variety of effects by our very presence, and when we actively decided to teach the kinds of content, writing and thinking – ways of seeing, and what Gayatri Chakravorty Spivak calls "worlding" – that we had to scream less to access, and so on. We have been able to provide some of what we needed – through our teaching, writing and general stubbornness – to some younger women in academic contexts. It is important to take stock of this because nobody else will, because it is part of mapping where we have been, part of recognising that as tired as we are, we continue to make inroads, to insist on an activist stance in South African academe. Over the last two years, I have become even more convinced of the importance of keeping this record of Black feminist women's contributions to the shifts in the academy – and elsewhere – as I heard several Black women professors maligned through a series of blatant lies that sought to wholesale erase the continued work they do. When such erasure has issued from those who themselves identify as feminist – regardless of race – I have been particularly devastated because I could not escape evidence of the transformative work these women had accomplished and continued to work at, in the face of a consistent backlash.

Clearly, there are ongoing challenges, some of which hit us in the face precisely because of some of the inroads we have and will continue to make. Some are the kicks of an old horse, which we hope is dying, and others are backlash. Bureaucracy is one of the new ways through which racism and sexist gatekeeping is enacted in South African academia, especially in the world of publishing. Stories of protracted underhanded dealings in the world of publishing abound for Blackwomen academics.

It is both a horrible and wonderful time to be in academia: wonderful because there is a small but un-silence-able community and we have changed some of the terms of discussion. In some respects we have grown up – and although still insurgent subjects, in the way that bell hooks uses it, we are no longer in the margins in the same kind of way that we were ten or fifteen years ago. At the same time, we have not taken over. I said it was both wonderful and horrible. It is horrible because in addition to the old familiar problems that exist in all untransformed environments, we now have to deal with newer problems we may not have anticipated.

The first of these comes from the onslaught of what I like to call the "homeland blacks", but not because they had the misfortune of living in homelands like some of us one day woke up and realised. These are not people who really come from the Transkei, Bophuthatswana, Venda, Ciskei (TBVC) states; they simply exhibit and embrace conservative politics reminiscent of the men who headed such projects. So, although we see more phenotypically Black bodies, academia's "homeland blacks" have the power-sharing mentality of a Sebe, a Buthelezi, a Mangope. Sometimes they have the *devious* conservativism of an Oupa Gqozo. When we were screaming and shouting about bringing in larger numbers of Black people in the academy, we forgot to think about how we would deal with conservative Black academics who are as anti-feminist as they are apologist for white supremacist epistemic projects.

Before we imagine that these people can be addressed in the same way that activists dealt with the Homeland leadership in the past, it might be worth noting that these techniques might be ineffective since some of the new generation of "homeland blacks" really do have power.

A second linked challenge for those academics among us who are interested in pursuing a genuinely transformative agenda is how to deal with the gate-keeping by the increasingly dangerous strata of conservative Blackmen, and women with the kinds of politics that made Desiree Lewis dub them phallic women over ten years ago. The danger with this kind is the struggle credentials that they often haul out as they take on increasing amounts of power and leadership positions in our academic institutions, assisting in the keeping out of Black people without money. A Black vice chancellor recently argued in favour of decreases to financial support for Black students at his Historically White University, claiming that we do not exist as Black academics.

As brilliantly coordinated as our effects have been in the academy, we have yet to rethink: what next? We are far from the powerless margins where we used to be. How, then, do we develop strategies that move beyond protesting and forcing our way in; how do we develop strategies for taking over? These continue to be challenging times, and we need to address these issues within academia as a matter of urgency.

At the same time, perhaps the strategies we so desperately need to develop to permanently alter the face of South African academia require that we pay attention to how far we have come, and the many ways we made sure we would arrive at this point. Our solutions may lie as much in our pasts as they do in our future innovations with weapons of struggle.

I was reminded that it is not only I who is excited by these presences. Two weekends before the UWC conference, a young feminist lawyer, whom I will refer to only as O, and I were introduced. She was very excited to meet me, and I, a little embarrassed, but I think it is important to speak about moments such as these because of what they illuminate. O's excitement was linked to what some of my words on page had allowed her to say and do in a context where she was rendered freak, highly othered in a university context where she was simultaneously not Black enough and too Black, treated as though she was a particularly spectacular – unusual, previously unseen, unAfrican – specimen given the xenophobic, homophobic, misogynist Black gatekeeping on that campus. Just as she was convinced that she was mad, developmental feminist mother notwithstanding, she took a feminist course that offered her the academic essays of many of the women doing feminist intellectual activist work. She pointed out that although she knew of the existence of many African feminists and womanist activists via her mother, most were older and all were activists outside academia. The discovery of the literature she was to read and revisit homed her.

This incident was very powerful for me at various levels. The encounter with O was important because it brought to the forefront several things about how we think. In the past, we deliberately set out to challenge the lies, gaps and absences in academia about Black subjectivities, experiences, ways of being and seeing, deliberately and consciously set out to dislocate comfortable Eurandrocentric interpretative authority, then and now. There have been some successes in this area. We have made some and continue to make a difference – to be what we needed to see in the world. Alice Walker speaks about writing what she wished she had been able to read, and deciding that there was not enough of it in the world. The film-maker Xoliswa Sithole once spoke powerfully about shining our light under the table when beaten down. She argues repeatedly and convincingly about the manner in which Blackwomen are conned into embracing "modesty" instead of owning our power, excellence and successes – and instead of openly celebrating each other's.

Our gains are not unimportant because we know that many feminists are still fighting to have these and other choices recognised as right in their respective countries. Professional women in the

US, I read recently, are still receiving considerably less payment for their services than the men colleagues similarly employed. The percentages of women academics at German universities are so low, in the single digits, that they make our situation appear heavenly. We know that even in those countries that lead with parliamentary representation, like Rwanda and South Africa, we do not live in a post-feminist state.

As we sat at the UWC gathering convened by Mary Hames, it was important to note that its existence and success was testimony to some of the way we had come. It was a time to celebrate ourselves. It was also a space to regroup, catch our breaths before we dived back into the heat of things as it were. I felt affirmed to walk the earth at the same time as the dangerous women that Grace Nichols evokes in the poem I cite. I remain grateful for the birthright Myesha Jenkins describes in her poem. Finally, I am confident that many more victories lie ahead, what with sisters who stare squarely in the face of danger and change the times.

CHAPTER 10

Winnie, Wambui, Wangari – on being difficult women

At the end of August 2011, news reached me that Wambui Waiyaki Otieno, the great revolutionary from Kenya, had died. I had never met her, and yet I felt a heavy loss, as though she was someone I had actually known intimately. Over the weeks that followed, I sat with my confusing sadness, and tried to make sense of it. It also marked the only time during which I could not write. My voice eventually returned, and I understood that my loss was linked to the hopelessness I was feeling that August as a South African woman. It was also linked to how vital the woman often called just Wambui has been to me as a feminist of the African world for over a decade.

I no longer remember why August 2011 had been so horrible. The specifics have faded from my memory and I do not care to google them. As I put the final touches to this book, in May 2017, South African news is saturated with how unsafe women are in my country. Several women's bodies have been found burnt beyond recognition after being killed by men they knew and possibly loved. Some of these men had been their lovers, while others killed them because these women chose women as lovers. The list of their names is so long, as feminists we find ourselves anxious about whose names are off the list. Before Karabo Mokoena was killed and burnt, possibly by her partner whom she had previously left for being abusive, there had been a two-week outcry over women being abducted along Oxford Road, a main road that runs through Killarney, Rosebank and Illovo, in Johannesburg by minibus taxi drivers who raped them. I say "possibly by her partner" because the news reports have changed almost daily on the details of this case. But Karabo Mokoena is still dead, cut down in the prime of her life, even though upon reporting her boyfriend's abuse to the police, she was turned away. I do not mean "alleged" by "possibly". I am confused only because news reports that he had confessed to killing and burning her were later retracted. I am not confused about what I believe and know about the frightening reality of intimate femicide in South Africa. Nor am I in doubt about the very real danger women face in their homes sometimes, and certainly every single time they leave their homes.

This perpetual sense of unsafety that I started to think about through my coinage "the female fear factory" or "the manufacture of female fear" in my last book, *Rape: A South African Nightmare*, is a very big part of what it means to live in a body recognisable as a woman's in this society.

Over the last three months, I have often walked into a lecture or tutorial room to teach some aspect of a contemporary African literary text – *Purple Hibiscus, Nervous Conditions, Men of the South* – and found my students in the middle of a group conversation about fear and the rawness of their feelings of pain. For many of my Black students, by the time I encounter them in the morning, they have already fought several battles just to get there. If they live off campus, they have dealt with sexual harassment as pedestrians, second-guessed their choices about which minibus taxi to take to campus, and practiced the vigilance our society rams down girls' and women's throats as a way to stay alive in our society. They have had to ask themselves, "is this a safe taxi?"

"Is this the taxi women were abducted and raped in?"

"Are there women in this taxi, and would any of them speak up if I were harassed?"

"Is this my last taxi ride?"

If they have been inappropriately touched by a stranger while fellow passengers looked away, shamed for their dress at a taxi rank, mugged on their way to or from campus in the past, they compartmentalise their pain in order to feel contained enough to make that daily journey to university in order to finish those degrees. Some of my men students speak of the real fear they experience every time they try to interrupt the public performance of violence. This interruption can turn deadly. It has turned deadly in a very prominent way in recent weeks when actor Mandla Hlatshwayo and his friend Oupa ChomChom Duma were shot by strangers as they tried to interrupt the mugging of two women outside Meli Lounge, a trendy pub in Pimville, Soweto in May 2017.

What does any of this have to do with Wambui Waiyaki Otieno, or Winnie Madikizela Mandela, or Wangari Maathai?

Everything. Given the constant onslaught of the many ways in which South African women are unsafe, I am not surprised that I no longer remember the specific public misogynist episodes in August 2011. The symbolic and embodied assaults on women's bodies and senses are relentless. It sometimes feels deliberately genocidal. In her comments on this manuscript, Grace Musila suggested that although femicide is always genocidal, "historically genocides have tended to be treated as male affairs, with women as incidental collateral damage, or spoils of patriarchal militaristic masculinities' tussles to hurt each other". I agree with her completely. However, whereas genocide suggests wiping a category of people off the face of the earth, femicide conjures up the killing of women *individually*. This has less to do with the etymology of each word, and more to do with public associations. I use genocidal here because I want to retain what femicide means and also the meaning of being under murderous attack as a group. For, as Musila reminded me, "femicide squarely locates the target and wounding on women's bodies", an association I intend here. However, "while genocide, even when women and children suffer the most, is often understood as a punitive gesture addressed to these women's men, and not to the women themselves", as Musila again reminded me, I want to destabilise this meaning through the evocation of genocidal femicide, which is what I intend here. Difficult women, like Wambui, Winnie and Wangari, stand as hopeful imagination against this fear and erasure of this mass femicide that I call genocidal above.

Wambui

From a physical distance, I have loved Wambui Otieno, Mau Mau, feminist, politician, first woman to run for public office in Kenya, unbowed woman ever since I have known about her. I followed her life – backwards and forwards – first, as the African feminist universe buzzed when she lost the legal battle to bury her husband where she wanted, then later reading a borrowed copy of her memoir, *Mau Mau's daughter* and afterwards stalking her online. I had alerts for every single time anything about her appeared online, and my Kenyan friends often sent me details I might have otherwise missed.

If it were not such a phallic metaphor, I would speak of Wambui as a tower, like a lighthouse of sorts, casting her light all around her at a dazzling world-changing pace, standing unbowed no matter the waves, standing steadfast as volcanoes and earthquakes shook the world beneath her feet.

That might very well be someone else's Wambui Waiyaki Otieno. However, I suspect that from the ancestral realm, she would frown at the limits of my imagination. Instead, I think of her more like a galaxy of possibilities. As she lived her life through increasingly unpredictable, but powerful choices, Wambui changed not just the world, but who we are in it too. When she joined Mau Mau as a teenager, and in later writing about those experiences in ways that challenge expectations, she drove home the importance of living our convictions. Although she could have settled into a life cushioned by class in colonial Kenya, she chose radical politics rather than the complicity of "safer" forms of resistance.

A girl and young woman raised in a middle-class family in colonial Kenya need not have run off to join the Mau Mau. There were other avenues of resistance available to her that would have enabled her to stay true to her convictions. The layers of complicated mythology around the Mau Mau would have been well known to her, as would the dangers of joining guerilla warfare. She made her choices.

After independence, her principles often brought her in collision with her former comrades. The stories of African nationalism are peppered with the names of women who have the backbone to differ radically with those they fought alongside. Pregs Govender. Nomfanelo Kota. Ruth First. Wambui Otieno spoke her truth regardless of the consequences. She stared danger in the face and not only spoke truth to power, but retained her revolutionary subjectivity in action.

Consistently.

She epitomised the personal as political and loved who she wanted to, shamelessly, and regardless of what those close to her thought. Bless her.

Ethnicity, class and age are all boundaries used to police who we may love on this continent, repeatedly. They are often ways of reminding women of what our place is.

When we are difficult women, the area of who we love, and how we love them, is the space through which we are often broken. The examples abound.

One: In that relentless pressure to partake in a lobola process you want nothing to do with. In the submission to emotional blackmail by those you love and from whom you come, eventually giving in to the process of being humiliated and put into place, reminded that you are *just a woman*. Even more painfully, as you try to live with yourself as hypocrite afterwards, unable to forgive yourself for agreeing to your own humiliation.

Two: The constant commentary about deviant women's sexual

behaviour. Why do you choose to call yourself lesbian when we know all the boyfriends from your past? How do you think it makes your ex-husband feel? Why are you so selfish? Why not just self-identify as a bisexual since that is safer and easier?

Cougar. Sugarmama. Desperate. So wild she cannot land a man of her own age and station in life. Shameful.

These tools are sjamboks used to discipline our spirits when we dare transgress the narrow limits of who society says we are. Wambui knew something about these, but she belonged to herself. A woman who belongs to herself is a wonder and a threat.

Oh, my heart, make me always a woman who belongs to herself. Yes, add to that Frantz Fanon's prayer too.

Wambui loved in independent Kenya as freely as she had scouted, spied, negotiated and carried arms for Mau Mau in colonial Kenya. She stood by her decisions and refused to be intimidated, no matter who stood against her. She survived her fiancé's betrayal that led to her imprisonment, attempted to sue her rapist as a way of holding him accountable in a world that said colonisers mattered and African women did not, loved her husband and comrade even though he was deemed the "wrong" ethnicity for her, fought his family in the legal and public courts to bury him where the couple had decided, and later married a man from a lower class who was also more than four decades younger.

Her heart kept her a woman who belonged to herself. In video clips, Wambui looks not only defiant but joyful. She lived her life on her own terms. And she inspired many of us to do the same: to live our truth, be unapologetic, and defend our revolutionary selves.

In the week Wambui Otieno died, I agreed to write about her for a supplement in a Kenyan paper alongside various feminists from different parts of the continent. I jumped at the opportunity to write about why she was important to me. For the first time in my life, words stayed away. A fortnight later, it hit me in the pit of my stomach. It is too soon, for I still needed her in the world.

Winnie

Many of us have a narrative of Winnie Mandela, whether it is comforting, anxiety-laden or a maddening story. Parts of that story have undoubtedly been influenced by her own choices, her self-representation, her utterances, her decisions on who to associate with, and so forth. At the same time, a large amount of what we know about her – as Winnie, as Winnie Mandela, as Winnie Madikizela-Mandela – comes to us mediated and remediated through wide-ranging circles of meaning-making.

A decade ago, before she and I were friends, I interviewed the socialist feminist filmmaker Xoliswa Sithole, Peabody winner and twice British Academy of Film and Television Arts (BAFTA) awardee, among numerous other accolades. In that interview, and various other times as she became one of my best friends, she told me that although she initially wanted to maintain a career in front of the camera, she decided to start making her own plays because of the paucity of the kinds of roles she wanted to play. She calls these "Angela Davis, Winnie Mandela kinds of roles".

She did not need to explain to me what she meant. I understood immediately what she was talking about – Black girl/woman to another, feminist to feminist. She wanted roles of women characters who have presence and voice. Such women are like Davis and Mandela: complicated, layered, uncontained women. She wanted roles that reflected women who were not a type: women who defied stereotype and patriarchal limitation. Roles of difficult women were so few and far between that Xoliswa Sithole decided she would no longer act; she would make films instead.

Winnie's complicated life is not for everybody. Sometimes, there are concerted efforts to make her smaller than she is. This, however, is not exclusive to the Winnie we see through her detractors.

In a 2013 article for *The New Yorker*, republished in a few British and US outlets, Nadine Gordimer wrote about Nelson Mandela, mourning his loss and recalling a specific conversation with him, told to her in a confidence the Nobel Laureate now felt justified breaking after his death. In that conversation, Gordimer recalled how devastated Nelson Mandela was by Winnie's affair with activist Dali Mpofu, or that she had lovers while he was incarcerated for twenty-seven years.

Gordimer's narrative is of a heart-broken husband, disappointed at what he assumed was a loyal, doting wife. Gordimer is aware of the many ways in which the expectation of fidelity to a spouse locked up for nearly three decades is highly gendered and difficult, if not impossible. Again, Musila's valuable interjection here was to remind me that Gordimer highlights how hers and Mandela's friendship is started off by her novel, *Burgher's Daughter*. After someone had snuck the novel into prison for Mandela, he had written her a letter about it. The novel, she says, is about the challenges of children of revolutionaries, living under daily threat of imprisonment. What is striking here, as Musila's feedback underscores, is the irony of Gordimer's lack of empathy and understanding for the burden of what Njabulo Ndebele in his novel *The Cry of Winnie Mandela* and Mamphela Ramphele in her scholarship had already described as political widowhood and its challenges. Musila wrote to me "in the piece, Gordimer chooses to recognise Mandela's human vulnerability to hurt; and in the novel, daughter's vulnerabilities, but not mothers and wives; who, it seems to her, remain locked in their roles as dutiful mothers and political widows". I had missed this connection, not having read this novel since my Honours dissertation on Gordimer submitted in 1994. However, I insert it here in gratitude for Musila's sharp literary critic eye. The hurt Musila highlights is muted in Gordimer's essay because hers is an attempt to speak about a different aspect of the statesman: the intimate life of her friend, to cast a light on aspects of his life that made him who he was, not just a heroic, saintly figure lost to the world.

But the novelist achieves so much more than this. She writes about Winnie in a very specific way: her failure to be a good wife. In order for Gordimer to fully sympathise with her friend's pain, she grapples with the source of his devastation: an unreasonable and yet real expectation of spousal fidelity in the face of a nearly three-decade absence. Gordimer must also be aware of the enduring fascination with "waiting" women in South Africa's political and literary cultures under apartheid. Often coded as "dutiful" wifehood, Mamphela Ramphele has much more aptly dubbed it "honorary widowhood".

What Winnie fails at here, and what devastates her husband, is dutiful wifehood and honorary widowhood. It should be unsurprising that the man who is written as legitimate national patriarch should be devastated by this failure. The expectation of dutiful wifehood is designed to buttress heroic nationalism. That is its function. However, Winnie "fails" because she refuses the burden of symbolism. She insists on being a messy, flesh and blood woman instead. Across the world, feminist scholarship have consistently illuminated that flesh and blood women pose a problem for nationalism since such women are interested in lives that are more than symbolic.

Many South African social media responses marked Gordimer's revelation as inappropriate: betrayal of confidence or a snide comment on Winnie that both placed unreasonable expectation and flattened her at a time when she needed sensitivity, and by some this was seen as an open attack on Winnie. Where Gordimer tried to shine a light on Nelson's (heteropatriarchal) devotion, her readers focused their attention on who such devotion works against.

What is interesting in this essay for me, in addition to Gordimer's full humanisation of her friend, Winnie Madikizela-Mandela's ex-husband, is the way in which Madikizela-Mandela appears here, not as herself, but as proxy for something else. Gordimer writes about Winnie in order to illustrate something that has very little to do with her.

The responses "in defence" of Winnie are not surprising because they echo her placement for many decades as "mother of the nation". This is after all what mothers of the nation are for: in different turns embrace and idolisation, on the one hand, and defence, on the other. But, Winnie is a difficult woman. She embraced and welcomed her status as "mother of the nation", but did so conditionally.

Let me move on to other narratives on her. In an article published on 1 July 1993 in *Weekly Journal*, Nokwanda Sithole presents a Winnie, "[w]iping the tears of a nation. Is this the future leader of South Africa? Defiant, beautiful and unbroken, Winnie Mandela remains one of the most powerful activists in the world." The Winnie that Sithole writes about here is an activist, strong, iconic figure who has some access to heroic presence, even if she also knows that heroic masculinity is a trap for women. For, although heroic nationalism requires some form of violence, this violence is often a blot against women. Heroic nationalism tells us in whose hands violence is permitted, and reminds us of its taboos in very gendered ways. Nokwanda Sithole invites us to ask what it means to be a soldier and whether imaginatively it is possible to be a woman soldier. Sithole knows there are actual women soldiers. That is not the question she invites us to grapple with, however.

Winnie's capacity for violence is the focus of Paul Trewhela's essay, in which he declares, "Mrs Mandela continues to provide the stuff of comment. She remains a formidable political force, despite her conviction for kidnapping the murdered Stompie Moeketsi Seipei, and three other youths, and the scandal concerning her private life."

Winnie Madikizela-Mandela's is a contested life, with mostly two dominant narratives. On the one hand, she is proxy-wife for the proper activist, heroic husband, which makes her part dutiful wife and part appendage. On the other hand, she is only murderous mother, the most offensive transgressor.

Yet her popularity and her stature as a subject of constant fascination also suggests that there are endlessly complicated ways to see her. She is difficult to trap in one stereotype or archetype. Monstrous mothers are lenses that can work as effectively as dutiful wife to contain women. Winnie Madikizela-Mandela remains uncontained in ways that challenge those who admire her as much as they unsettle those who demonise her.

Given how effectively women are erased from memory of struggle and absented from official nationalist narrative, Winnie's endurance is a significant study in bucking the norm in ways resistant to explanation.

Wangari

Wangari Maathai is the kind of African woman the meritocrats love to reference. We are invited to celebrate her as part of celebrating African excellence. Looking at her life, it is not hard to see how a consistent overachiever has more than enough evidence to support this narrative.

Not only was she the first woman in East and Central Africa to graduate with a PhD in 1971, she went on to teach veterinary anatomy at the University of Nairobi for a few years before clinching two more firsts – as Head of Department in 1976, and professorship in 1977. The Nobel Laureate for Peace and founder of the Greenbelt Movement, whose radical Pan Africanist and feminist environmentalist politics did not always translate well across borders, repeatedly highlighted why taking care of the environment was a multi-layered political project.

In her highly publicised speeches, she insisted that women were closer to the earth in many African contexts, not because of the essences that colonial and African patriarchies mythologise, but due to their burden of agricultural and domestic work, both of which depended on the health of the earth. Therefore, she reasoned, women see environmental degradation first. And, as she built and led a movement that crossed borders of ethnicity, generation and nation state, her work's real impact is something we will fully appreciate long after her death.

In her brilliant essay 'Silence is a woman', Wambui Mwangi relates a little known story outside of Kenya:

> In 1992, Wangari Maathai led a group of women that occupied "Freedom Corner" in Nairobi's Uhuru Park, demanding the release of political prisoners arrested and detained by the Moi regime. The government sent armed police to evict the women,

who stripped naked in protest and defiance. Wangari Maathai was beaten unconscious and hospitalized, but the women of Freedom Corner won eventually.

The Wangari Maathai in the above excerpt is both similar to, and radically different from, the Nobel Laureate so beloved of the global environmentalist movement. She is defiant and unbowed, with an unshaken commitment to social justice. The intersections between her work in the academy and in social movements were clear to her. She engaged in feminist strategy by taking the meaning of African land as linked to African women's realities to its logical ends.

Daniel arap Moi's police recognised how dangerous she and her comrades were, and they sought to punish her with the violence all radical political activists recognise. Mwangi locates this form of women's national protest in a long line of anti-colonial women's public activism, which is either mythologised or tidied out of Kenyan nationalist narrative, where even revolutionary women are discursively rendered as "safe" and silent. The hypocrisy Mwangi highlights lies in the violence with which radical women's activism is treated. Yet, states always know that these women are not safe if we look at responses to women's activism in the above story as well as comparative contexts.

Celebration is often a double-edged sword for exceptional and difficult women. It is often haunted by an attempt to render such women more compliant, erasing those aspects of their choices and lives that cannot be tidied into celebratory narratives. Maathai spoke repeatedly against attempts to limit women, reasserting in different sites her consistent decolonialist environmental feminism. Furthermore, she surfaced the complicated intimate life partnerships that come with such iconic status in her autobiographical writing.

Far from representing an ideal to be emulated and venerated, Wambui Waiyaki Otieno, Winnie Madikizela-Mandela, Wangari Maathai lived complicated lives that offer both warning and inspiration. In very different ways, they each illustrate the work transgressive femininities perform in the world, and the limits of heroism for women. While each has been celebrated, all of them have also consistently chosen to exceed the categories of celebrated women. Their successful resistance against attempts to render them safe – be it through policing their romantic and/or sexual desire, their shifting relationships to nationalist projects, or their failure to conform to regimes of containment – offer freeing visions of unsubjugated femininities.

CHAPTER 11

Writing African feminists

Celebrating FEMRITE at 20

I first heard of FEMRITE, the Uganda Women Writers' Association, a few months after it was formed in 1996, and although it represented such exciting possibility even then, I marvel at the successes of the institution's ability to not only survive, but grow from strength to strength over the last two decades. Two decades later, given the volumes of writing and the successful publishing model, the legacy that FEMRITE continues to build exceeds those very early brave hopes and plans.

In its early years, I remember how highly it figured in discussions at a workshop we had on SAWPI – short for the South African Women's Press Initiative – the brainchild of the feminist poet Roshila Nair, who has some publishing background, and feminist literary scholar and cultural theorist, Desiree Lewis. SAWPI hoped to chart the way to the launch of a South African Women's Press, bemoaning the decline of the independent publisher and closing of previous women's presses in South Africa.

Although SAWPI was not to be, although it did not become like FEMRITE or Modjadji or Cassava Republic, three powerful testimonies to the possibilities of African feminist publishing, I am thrilled that I have all three to name as leaders in publishing and disseminating the most exciting writing coming out of the African literary landscape today.

But FEMRITE really came most alive – and not just as an exciting idea – for me when I met Monica Arac de Nyeko and Beatrice Lamwaka for the first time at a conference on literary studies in South Africa in the early days. I gathered some of the earlier FEMRITE publications and delved into them, copies of which I still mostly have. I have lost some, but I know I am not the only person whose books seem to grow legs. I remember the delightful title *Men love chocolate, they just don't admit it*.

I have returned to the collections of short stories and novels first discovered on that encounter, and have been able to expand my collection of FEMRITE books since then. Both Monica Arac de Nyeko and Beatrice Lamwaka have since grown to have illustrious literary careers, with important awards, and their works studied across the world. I am not crediting FEMRITE for their talent. However, I wonder how much longer it would have taken for us to learn all their short stories about the relationships between history, sexuality, pleasure, same-sex desire and the fluidity of identity, had they not been members of FEMRITE. How much poorer would we have been had de Nyeko's 'Jambula Tree' and Lamwaka's 'Chief of the Home' never been published?

One of my favourite texts to read and teach is by another member of FEMRITE. Doreen Baingana's *Tropical Fish* is a collection I have taught for almost a decade in different guises. I love watching my students fight over which sister makes the most sense/which one they like the most/who most reflects them. They are never dispassionate about the sisters. I still have the three versions with Mustafa Maluka covers that were issued in South Africa because I *had to* have all three.

I have only been to Uganda once in my life, to attend the twentieth anniversary of FEMRITE. Yet, it is a literary and publishing presence that has been very important to me as an African feminist in a different part of the continent. I know how hard it is to build lasting feminist institutions. I am familiar with the thankless work, the endless demands and the burn out, all while pushing back against the patriarchal deligitimation and financial challenges. And feminists are human, so not all working relationships are productive even with the greatest commitment.

I am interested in the African feminist literary imagination, the world that FEMRITE enters, and the world that this institution has helped shape for over two decades. By African feminist imagination I refer to a range of expressions of creative agency that deconstruct patriarchal power. These suggest new possibilities, informed by the widespread understanding within academic disciplines (literary scholarship, art history, fine arts, musicology, film and television studies, media studies) that study creativity with the conviction that creative texts offer a space where "newness enters the world" to borrow Homi Bhabha's formulation. Indeed, much critical work within the Humanities points to the manner in which creative genres usher in possibilities that are oftentimes elusive in other more straightforward commonsensical discourses. African feminist imagination denotes and resides in the evocative, the suggestive, the world of the experimental.

It is volatile. It is customary to speak of women in terms of water metaphors, but I resort to metaphors of fire and volatility because the African feminist imagination is explosive against patriarchal doublespeak. The words used by participants in an African feminist project are loaded words: fiery, explosive, suggestive, adaptive and risky.

The loaded, volatile worlds I evoke, therefore, are not militaristic violent metaphors, but are, in fact, informed by a logic against war, as Nelson Maldonado might say. The logic of war is so pervasive after the violent nightmare of slavery, colonialism, apartheid and structural adjustment, it is often hard to conceptualise forms of contestation uncontained by the dominion of war. Yet, everywhere around us, there is evidence of other manifestations of loaded words to wound and to empower. The African feminist imagination is not just the product of cultural workers and activists who self-identify as feminist, although it does create a feminist public consciousness. Rather, the African feminist imagination is what the productive collision of writing women and rioting women births, to borrow a concept from the African feminist literary scholar Susan Andrade. After Andrade, we can observe that dominant feminist scholarship from outside the continent has taken for granted that to study women's movements in political science or sociology has nothing to do with studying women's literary writing, except to read them for information, mining them for context. It also holds that the novels feminists write borrow from scholarship and knowledge created in more straightforwardly "factual" narratives in non-fiction. Of course, non-fiction is not any less creative or loaded whether produced in the academy or elsewhere. In other words, the bulk of scholarship outside of African feminist lenses proceeds as though, on the one hand, we need to look at rioting women – the protesting, marching, lobbying, petitioning, jailed, prosecuted and criminalised women – as exhibiting a form of legitimate but raw agency that is ripe for interpretation but usually cannot theorise itself. Rioting women are the bodies in the streets. Writing women, on the other hand, are the middle-class educated writer women who theorise in writing, resisting patriarchal oppression in their own name. For African feminist literary critics and literary historians, this distinction has been enormously unhelpful. Instead, we insist on reading writing women as rioting women, largely because this makes sense against the backdrop of women who were activists and strategists, some of whom went on to write.

The substantial body of women activist biographies in various parts of the continent – Wambui Waiyaki Otieno, Wangari Maathai, Winnie Mandela, Mamphela Ramphele as some of the better-known ones – have made it impossible to continue as though these categories of women are separate. To read writing women as rioting women is, first, to recognise that these identities are not mutually exclusive. They can very often be mutually reinforcing.

Sometimes the same concrete historical subject partakes in both, as Maathai did throughout her life. It makes no sense, then, to imagine that the persona of a writing, theorising, strategising Prof Maathai was completely distinct from the embodied, marching, protesting, tree-planting Maathai who was often physically assaulted for her politics. Indeed to imagine such a split in the same person is ridiculous. When former Kenyan president Daniel arap Moi's soldiers beat her up, they had no care for her PhD and theorising capacity. They saw a dangerous, defiant, protesting woman, as Wambui Mwangi teaches us.

Second, it is to reject the idea of writing as safe and rioting as dangerous; to recognise the power of women's writing in our contexts. As African feminist literary scholars, we insist on reading imaginative agency in the material resisting cultures whether textual or embodied as theorising, partly in flagrant disregard for the pressure to reinscribe the Cartesian or Enlightenment logic that posits the body of knowledge docile to interpretation, which is an epistemic reinscription of how African raw material is docile and ready for processing elsewhere to ready it for easy/ready consumption. It is not possible to hold on to an idea of writing as safe against the background of South African Miriam Tlali's consistent banning or Egyptian Nawal el Sadaawi's detention. These African feminists were not treated as people engaged in safe activity by the regimes that recognised how loaded and revolutionary their work was. Miriam Tlali buried dozens of books in her backyard in Soweto because she understood both how precious the written word is, as a writer herself, and how deadly the consequences of being found with the wrong book could be in apartheid South Africa.

Loaded words come with risk – sometimes debilitating risk, and at other times fertile risk. They are also always haunted by tone-deafness and counter-accusations of illegitimacy.

When we talk about reading cultures, the worlds of the imagination, and the possibilities of literature, we enter the terrain of loaded words, unapologetically so and dangerously so at the same time. Loaded words are saturated and weighed down with layers and layers of meaning. Like onion skin, glistening, sensual, frustrating, powerful, tear-inducing, delicious. We are confronted with the many ways in which, historically, words and the imagination have been at the heart of making the world we now inhabit. They have inscribed value and they have legitimised harm and degradation. In other words, although this is often contested, we are aware of long histories in which words have materiality.

Literacy and more specifically low literacy rates are often thrown at us when we argue about the importance and materiality of words and the power of the imagination. It has become an axiom to insist that literacy levels impede the movement of literary texts in African contexts, although I imagine that given East African reading cultures and histories, this warning is issued in a manner less brazen there than it is in southern Africa.

Nonetheless, the paradox of African literary production is a double-expectation: on the one hand, we are expected, especially as women who occupy the literary space, to recognise as valid the claims that literature is key to resistance – indeed many anti-colonial and nationalist movements insisted on literature as a weapon for our collective freedom – and on the other, accept that we should temper our wild ambitions to be read since most Africans apparently do not read. This is some of the load that comes with being a woman of words, a woman interested in the worlds of words and what they can create.

This is the first meaning of loaded words I intend; the burden that the collision of gender and history bring to literary women, the burden to work to prove that women's writing, women's publishing, can flourish and that it can change the way we think about literary value. The load literary women have to carry is like the seven mountains Molara Ogundipe-Leslie uses to speak about how African women negotiate subjectivity, moving with seven mountains on our backs, not heroic or stoic but for ourselves, in service of a vision that expands our realms of possibility. This is the world of African feminist literary work – the work that contributes to the feminist imagination.

Loaded words can explode our conceptions of ourselves

and our worlds. To be a literary woman is to wade through the supposedly well-meaning cautionary words – be careful, do not dream too ambitiously, there are not enough readers, there isn't enough time, the work is thankless – words laced with less well-intentioned doubt and sometimes sabotage.

Yet we know that when literacy is learnt through literature, literature is seminal to the construction of resistance and to ushering in the new. This is evident when we recognise but also reject the ways in which language is often restricted to functionalist use that locks it only into answering "how does this allow me to do that?". This functionalist use excludes literary, imaginative power because it pre-empts what language can do, what words can do, as finite, limited, static.

Such functionalist prescription obscures how writing is the realm of the imagination, dreaming and learning to understand the world. Academic discourse is often seen as not having much power in the world – except in the case of financial disciplines, hard sciences and technology. Reading is treated disrespectfully and not seen as engaging complexly with ideas and the world. Yet, we know that empathy is an effect of critical thinking.

The burden of defending the work of writing as valid is also linked to that of recognising the importance of reading complexly. FEMRITE along with many other sites that produce, defend, surface and circulate the African feminist imaginative project have been unapologetic in insisting on reading complexly.

How, you may ask.

The invitation – or indeed the challenge – of reading complexly cannot be divorced from the production of material that is not effortless, that does not choose the trouble-free way out. To expand the feminist imagination, to insist on complex reading requires the production of "texts that are volatile in their relationship to the world in order to engage with the world", to use AC Fick's formulation, because "in reading creative texts, there is a suspension of self as central and therefore a challenge to your sense of self". In old fashioned literary critical vocabulary, this is what we call "the suspension of disbelief". This is the temporary forgetting that characters are fictional and separate from us, the ability to feel empathy or contempt or whatever other feeling the author provokes; to believe in their thoughts, emotions and experiences as though they come from concrete historical subjects (or people). But Fick intends more than the suspension of disbelief, pointing as he does to how loaded words are in remaking us as well.

Fick continues to outline how each encounter with a volatile text is "a different confrontation". This means that reading a novel or short story or literary essay twice creates a different exchange, taking you to a different place. And each encounter with texts engaged in a volatile relationship with their world (and yours as reader) develops the ability to decode increasingly complex narratives – not just those rendered in self-consciously creative realms, but those beyond in the worlds of concrete historical subjects. Intertextuality is learnt in the doing, by doing, in praxis, in context. Meanings are obvious or obscured based on what kinds of intertextual readings we have been exposed to or confronted by previously. In a context where the brain's elasticity has been trained for functionality – or to only recognise a static set of truths/realities/possibilities – it becomes harder to read the layers of meaning and possibilities. Yet volatile, loaded words can threaten this stability, exploding its borders.

The Guyanese British feminist writer Grace Nichols insists that language is a site of embattlement. In her essay titled 'The battle with language', she reflects on writing in ways that are both pleasurable and deviant (volatile) for a feminist writer. She ends her essay with the declaration "it is the battle with language that I love", in a way reminiscent of the end of her classic collection *I is a long memoried woman* which ends "I have crossed an ocean/I have lost a tongue/from the root of the old one/a new one has sprung". Nichols is speaking as a feminist writer of the African diaspora, but I do not think that what she describes here is radically different from the challenges facing those of us who write as feminist from the African continent in the late twentieth and early twenty-first centuries.

African feminist imagination demands the refashioning of

new languages again and again, in conversation, taking risks, unlearning, unburdening and reloading.

To enter the literary world is to enter a landscape of words as landmines. Literary scholars have shown the ways in which, across the continent, patriarchal literary cultures have entrenched masculinist ways of representing women characters. The extensive work of feminist literary scholarship has only begun to indent the masculine business-as-usual of the African masculine literary canon, as taught, as framed in terms of fathers and founders, nation and tradition. Motherhood, women's sexuality, and widowhood, although all highly visible, exist in much canonical men's writing in the realm of the symbolic. Historically, women characters were rendered in a complicated matrix that appeared to celebrate while obscuring (motherhood), contain and demonise (sexuality) and placing women as proxies for missing men (widowhood), re-entering and re-centring the missing dead or detained or disappeared husband when confronted with women's behaviour patterns, rather than taking women's agency and the project of representing women characters seriously. In other words, re-centring heroic masculinism and to make women "stand in figures for men" in Samuelson, Musila and Lewis' terms. These tropes have not only dominated nationalist literary cultures, they retained their grip on political public discourse alongside notions of respectability. By motherhood, I am not just referring to the "mother Africa" trope in which generations of African men writers fashioned women characters who suffered stoically, barely spoke except as miniature representations of the nation, supporting the men they were attached to through marriage, suffering endlessly on behalf of the children they bore, and dying. The mother Africa trope – as we now know, thanks to established and interdisciplinary African feminist criticism – is a way of making women characters stand in for what was done to the continent: raped, pillaged, trampled on, impoverished, bled dry, robbed, all while the character itself may not speak back. But women are not continents. The reduction of motherhood to the symbolic in nationalist imaginative projects and writing also mythologised motherhood at the same time that mothering is erased (and women who mother) are erased, brutalised and trivialised. Motherhood is a trope in much African writing that works against women and women's varied subjectivities, requiring what Sibongile Ndashe calls "passwords" before women can write in their own name.

In August 2016, on my way from Entebbe airport, to Kampala, my taxi driver, with whom I had a most enjoyable conversation, played Juliana's popular song 'Woman'. It was interesting to me how many times he referred to her narrative, her lyrics as being about African mothers. As I made him replay the song and video I was struck by how the lyrics subscribed to and challenged hypervisible patriarchal constructions of women. Juliana's woman is superhuman: she smiles in the face of pain, evoking the strong Blackwoman or stoic African woman trope; she is both courageous and hyper-feminine, in line with expectations of women's availability for heterosexual consumption culture; she has superhuman strength that sees her work tirelessly, smile when in pain and repress a frown.

However, listened to in full, Juliana's song suggests multiple women, rather than one woman. Even though some of the lyrics in Juliana's song mention both motherhood and womanhood, the driver conflated them. Juliana sings "Her womanhood and her motherhood/Are her strength and pride" in a part of the song that is about celebrating the woman's sense of personal style and "state of mind". Described as "beautiful", possessing grace, with attraction to beautiful, colourful clothing, this woman is a mother, but this is certainly not the most significant part about her. Interestingly, this is the only part of the song that mentions the subject as a mother. Indeed, the chorus gestures to a more complicated reading of the woman in question, repeating "A warrior is a woman ... A saviour is a woman". Her "magic" in the song lies in her capacity to bravely navigate fear and adversity. Motherhood appears only once.

Yet, although he was choosing not to listen to the lyrics of the song he admitted to playing regularly, the taxi driver was not entirely imaginative in his conflation of mother and woman.

Interestingly, Juliana's song is generally about women. It is my taxi driver's decision to insert African.

It was still not a coincidence that he slipped into "mother" where the lyricist retained "woman". These representations are mutually reinforcing. Motherhood is celebrated in ways that rhyme with strong Black/African women in historic ways, but also ways that endure.

And so, decades ago, confronted with the question: how does a woman writer write motherhood and characters engaging motherhood against this backdrop, the writers Flora Nwapa and Buchi Emecheta answer: she cannot. She has to unbundle and un-write it. She has to kill it. In their novels, Nwapa's *Efuru* and Emecheta's *The Joys of Motherhood*, they write of women characters who must come to adulthood with no mothers – or with mothers who are dead at the beginning of their novels. And after Susan Andrade's scintillating African feminist reading of these two novels together, we begin to see this killing of metaphoric mothers as part of writing the difficulty of late twentieth-century African femininity. It is how Nwapa and Emecheta theorise the absence of a ready literary tradition that homes women. In other words, Emecheta and Nwapa before her insist that an African feminist literary tradition needs to birth itself; that it cannot rely on the terms of the African men's literary canon, nor can it benefit from accepting honorary male status, or assume all women's imaginative spaces are there for its benefit. Through Andrade's reading of their work, we begin to see how together they inaugurate an African feminist literary tradition on terms that are very different from that of their men peers. Efuru, raised as honorary man and the favourite child of a politically and economically powerful man must nonetheless experiment in relationships with other women and men. Because her deviant, marriage-shunning, unbowed mother dies in childbirth, Efuru grows up with an interrupted connection to this lineage of deviant women, and unbounded femininities. Consequently, she must create her own future, stumbling along, sometimes misrecognising patriarchal pedestals for power. In Emecheta's novel, as in Nwapa's before hers, mothers are everywhere engaged in the complicated joyful, exhausting, challenging, rewarding business of mothering. But motherhood is absent. Yet, Andrade suggests provocatively that when she opens her novel with the closing words of Nwapa's, Emecheta invites a reading of Nwapa's as the original text, the mother text. A tradition of provocative reading, loading words with ideas that expand.

I could just as easily have made a similar argument about intertextuality, literary lineages and feminist imagination in Chimamanda Ngozi Adichie's *Purple Hibiscus* and Tsitsi Dangarembga's *Nervous Conditions*. Taking a cue from Adichie's opening line and early interviews, much scholarship has read Adichie's debut novel as being in conversation with Achebe's own debut novel. However, there is much evidence to support reading *Purple Hibiscus* as a novel that is in conversation with another novel of the African (and) feminist tradition: *Nervous Conditions*. Adichie extends both Achebe and Dangarembga in productive ways. She provides a counterpoint to Achebe's protagonist, Okonkwo – whose battle with masculinity is cast through authorial sympathy *and* leads to his demise – in Aunty Ifeoma, the sister of Eugene, Adichie's Okonkwo figure. Ifeoma is her brother's equal in social stature, makes different personal and political decisions and makes it possible for readers of Adichie's novel to read Eugene's tyranny as chosen patriarchal tyranny, rather than just inherited brutality. Linked to this, Adichie echoes the intergenerational tension of Achebe's novel between fathers and sons. However, she takes it further than Achebe since her character Jaja actively challenges the father's tyranny and refuses patriarchal masculinity, rather than simply "failing" at masculinity like Achebe's Nwoye.

While Dangarembga creates a novel with multiple stagings of femininity, all of which are plagued with considerable difficulty, and refuses the celebration of motherhood with Lucia as the sole joyful transgressor in *Nervous Conditions*, Adichie writes no "community of women". There is no burden of motherhood, although mothering is complicated by both Dangarembga and Adichie. Aunty Ifeoma offers a model of a dynamic African femininity and its rewards for Kambili, Adichie's girl protagonist, whose own mother is complicatedly flawed. In other texts within the African feminist literary canon, a chosen sisterhood is written as connection rather than motherhood, as we see in a novel like Mariama Bâ's *So Long a Letter*, for example.

However, if women writers repeatedly imagine complicated women's and girls' subjectivities in their novels, public nationalist discourses on motherhood survive and leak into readings of popular culture, as my encounter with the taxi driver partly illustrates.

Representations of women as mothers are not the only ways in which the African male literary canon cemented limiting representations of women. Widowhood and sexual desire have also been powerful ways to write African women characters in ways that stage what Gabeba Baderoon has called ambiguous visibility. The control of women's sexuality is as key in literature as it is in public political discourse across many countries. It is an obsession with keeping women in place; it controls women's movement. The demonisation of women's free will, physical movement in and into urban areas, and overall autonomy that we see translating into the stereotype of the urban woman as whore in Zimbabwean literature that Rudo Gaidzanwa traces echoes public discourse after the first chimurenga. Equally, the obsession with "whorish" women in much South African creative culture has much to do with how women are increasingly forging economically viable lives in ways that contravene respectability politics; while the public censure and shaming of women like Vera Sidikaa is not unlinked to the public outcry over how unbounded but also heroic women like Wambui Otieno chose lives of their own in Kenya previously.

In other words, while the scholarship has long lashed the rendering of the African woman's sexuality as corrective terrain, these ideas and patriarchal senses of entitlement retain their grip on the public imagination. They remain trapped in Baderoon's "ambiguous visibility".

Ambiguous visibility is a violent exercise of loaded words, loaded imagery. It is the high circulation of an oppressed figure or products from her in ways that render her invisible. In other words, while there is much ink spilt on describing women – or women characters – they are under control, acted on, described, and so, we are invited to look at them, rather than be challenged to engage them. Ambiguous visibility is a concept Baderoon coins to describe how the gaze – male gaze, white gaze – packages and neutralises African characters and cultural activity. In other words, it is a sophisticated form of erasure where what you see the most is invisibilised and rendered safe and consumable as such.

In the minds, mouths and on the pages of African feminist writing, loaded words are the terrain of authority and contesting authority. From FEMRITE, we continue to learn how to craft spaces of authority imaginatively, how to explode the boundaries of genre and value of high/low culture.

Doreen Baingaina speaks in one of her essays, as well as in her TEDx talk, of the layers of meaning and being we need to negotiate in order to navigate words that harm and offend, opposing censorship, and imagining ourselves into new identities, new pleasures and new freedoms. African feminist imagination, she reminds us, is risky, volatile terrain. It is necessary. It comes with responsibility to unburden ourselves and others and reload words with new meanings that expand what counts as literature.

Hers is a pointer to how literature theorises, like some of the writers I have mentioned above, and many, many more I haven't. Like Calixthe Beyala whose beautiful women characters own their libidinous, leaking bodies, speak for themselves and defend each other. Like Danai Mupotsa whose scholarship and poetry is an exercise in writing in fire. There is no contradiction between the imaginative and theoretical. Indeed, as many African feminist literary scholars alongside Andrade, such as Nnaemeka, Lewis, Musila and others have insisted, engagement with African feminist literary production requires that we read imaginative texts as also engaged in the work of theorising what is possible and desirable. This is part of the terrain FEMRITE chooses to traverse.

If FEMRITE entered two decades ago this world of loaded words as burden, it has chosen to disrupt, evoke, embolden and revolutionise how we think about reception. In her work, Lynda Gichanda Spencer draws extensively on FEMRITE writers to build an argument about the shifting face of women's writing and the work of unmaking and reshaping genre. Whereas literary scholarship globally has proceeded along lines that have opposed what is called "women's popular fiction" (and within that chick lit) to "literature proper", she demonstrates the ways in which FEMRITE is at the leading edge of literature that pays no attention to these divisions. Indeed, as Spencer shows with East and Southern African writers, there has emerged a genre and generation of women writers who carve highly political literature that is at the same time sophisticatedly weaving contemporary aesthetics into its fabric. Not for these writers, safety in domesticity, avoidance of the political and the reinscription of patriarchal femininities. Instead, repeatedly, the East African women writers Spencer analyses, like the West African urban literary traditions Lydie Moudileno focuses on, push us to rethink what we know about literature, how to write about women, how to speak African Literature, the new faces of African literature, what political writing looks like, who decides, how to publish and ascribe value, and what no longer works for us.

Rising to meet these questions, African feminist literary and cultural scholars such as Lydie Moudileno, Lynda Gichanda Spencer and Dina Ligaga suggest that these bodies of literature usher in new literary insights that can transform what we think of as African literature's boundaries. They redefine how genre works within bodies of women's literature anywhere, while examining how women's imagination in the African world challenges just about anything we think we knew before the current explosion. Taking seriously African women's worldviews opens up creative universes, political analyses, and ultimately reforms genres.

It also blurs and sometimes explodes the relationships between the popular and high cultural sites and forms of imaginative output, pushing us to rethink the urban and reflect in more sustained ways about the meeting places of intimacy and history in African life; a project exquisitely rendered in Lilia Momple's novel, *Neighbours: The Story of a Murder* as well as Baingaina's prose and Adichie's fiction.

It is a time when the African feminist imaginative landscape also invites revisiting feminist traditions, rethinking connections between sisters. One of the most enduring attributes of African women's writing is the refusal to think about connections and intimacy between women as reliant on sameness. Difference is used to portray not only strength and vitality, but to illuminate and enrich, an approach to difference (as strength) that is also a key distinguishing factor of African feminism as many of us have long argued.

FEMRITE writers more recently have challenged us to start imagining the knottiness of intimacy, and what friendships, love, histories and futures look like. In a project allied but also radically different from her peer, Monica Arac de Nyeko's award-winning short story 'Jambula Tree', Beatrice Lamwaka in one of her short stories 'Chief of the Home' forces us to think about how histories matter.

Loaded words are also how, as African women, we write ourselves out of despair.

Discussions in Southern Africa on publishing and the literary world today are stuck in negotiating how to decolonise the structures and distribution networks of literary production, boycotting, creating and recreating alternatives, moving beyond established reference points, not believing the pronouncements of the limitations of reading patterns, what we know vs what we think we know.

At the same time, as a Southern African woman who is animated by the explosion of daring, visionary, volatile feminist vision and young feminist activist energy today, I am also struck by how invisibilised the work of previous generations of women's movements is. Growing up in apartheid South Africa, I was aware of various defiant, out of control women in the vein of Winnie Mandela, and Federation of South African Women (FEDSAW), Skottaville Press, Cheryl Carolus, National Organization for Women (NOW) and the powerful Zimbabwean women's movement. To live in a post-apartheid Southern Africa in which radical women's imagination is cast as without history, as the first –

rioting and writing – is puzzling. It is puzzling when we consider 1in9 campaign, the organisation put together to support the complainant in the Zuma rape trial. The writing rioting purple shirts were often carried out of court, bodies twisted by the police, who stood against the thousands of men and women bussed in to support the accused Zuma who would later become president. There is also #RapeAtAzania where #RhodesMustFall activists rejected police inaction when one of their own was raped in what should have been a safe space, and instead circulated the rapist's name and photo on social networks. Although the police could not on their own track him down, people worked together to find him so he could be arrested. We also have #RUReferenceList that listed the names in an attempt to contest the notion that rape culture did not exist on university campuses or that university authorities were acting to curb it.

To be an African feminist writing, rioting woman on the continent is to be engaged in constant self-defence against erasure of an African feminist tradition, to begin anew, to be invited to refer to first/second/third waves which obscure and deny the long presences of African feminist movements and imagination.

In *A Renegade Called Simphiwe* and in subsequent academic articles, I have sketched a figure I call "The New South African Woman" or NSAW for short. She is usually assumed to be educated, and her body is in line with contemporary mainstream notions of a worked-at, beautiful woman, with the requisite body and hairstyling choices. She lives at the right address because of the cultural capital it communicates (even if this lifestyle is unaffordable to her), she consumes the most visibly fashionable reading and designer products. She is assertive and moderated and committed to heteropatriarchal romance epitomised by (sustaining) marriage.

Importantly, the NSAW embodies and performs women's empowerment in public arenas but offers clear evidence of conventional femininity as performed in private. I summarise the NSAW here, but recognise similar aspects in conventional femininity pressures in several other urban African contexts.

As women located in contemporary Africa who do not want to

be bullied into this vision, which is further reduced to the realm which cannot be rendered into real high literature, FEMRITE has offered us a vision of ourselves that charts new paths. It is possible to write about contemporary Africa in ways that are pleasurable and disruptive, as FEMRITE writers do, to expand the realm of what counts as political.

In her unpublished presentation at the FEMRITE@20 conference, Gloria Mwaninga reminded us that as global citizens and human beings on the planet, we can draw from whatever we want, that feminisms from elsewhere are as much a resource for us as what we craft for ourselves. She is right, of course. However, given the unequal power in global relations, we often also have to defend our gains from credit claimed elsewhere. When media and scholarship battle to explain how Chimamanda Ngozi Adichie's or NoViolet Bulawayo's or Panashe Chigumadzi's feminisms are possible; how Binyavanga Wainaina's, K Sello Duiker's or Chris Abani's queer literary projects are possible, they often insist on looking outside the continent to explain the volatile feminist imagination of these continentally-born and raised writers who are among the most celebrated globally today.

In other words, this is an attempt to write a literary history that shows how feminism is foreign to Africanness. We must recognise FEMRITE's successes on meeting the largesse and boldness of its vision, defending its legacies as it continues to fashion and extend them. It should not make sense to write a literary history of contemporary queer and/or feminist writing that does not recognise the work that FEMRITE and its allies do, in the expansion of the African feminist imagination by creating not only alternative public spheres, but worlding anew, as Gayatri Spivak might say. Loaded words are also about remaking a/the world, what Spivak writes of as wording/worlding or wor(l)ding.

Reading FEMRITE's contribution to the African literary world, to the African feminist universe as linked to Cassava Republic, to Modjadji underscores both the openings in publishing and what we are able to do in literary studies now. We are able to: rise to the challenge of making sense of, reading, and being transformed by the kinds of literary and political interventions and creations that Moudileno, Ligaga and Spencer write of. We live at a time when to think of African literature with attention to the present requires that we pay attention to the centrality of intertwined gender, sexuality and imagination. At a time when despite – or maybe because of – the precarity of queer existence, some of the most expansively visionary fictional engagements with sexuality, intimacy and power are coming from East Africa.

I cannot imagine that it is a coincidence that such brilliantly transformative work is coming from the place that also produced the most significant output by women writers, that set out to transform publishing and succeeded. It is no coincidence that one bold vision enables another. FEMRITE writers "have constantly pushed the boundaries of convention and dared to widen the horizons of the possible with regards to socially prescribed gendered behaviour", to borrow Grace A Musila's words from another essay.

I am thrilled to benefit from the firing up of the imagination.

More than just responding to existing traditions – resisting, expanding, writing back – FEMRITE's has not been a single, tidy, controlled narrative. It is one that writes and riots us out of containment.

CHAPTER 12

My mother's daughter, my sons' mother

For many years, like millions of women across the world, I voraciously read women's magazines. I read them in the way I imagined that most readers do: in a combination of fascination and distance from some of what they espoused. I read them selectively but was obviously not immune to their seduction.

One of themes they returned to was that of mother-daughter relationships. As someone who has been very close to her mother for most of my life, this was an area I could not completely understand. Popular cultural sites targeted at young-adult women often frame the mother-daughter relationship as a difficult one. They endlessly recycle the gospel that turning into our mothers is something to fear, and the notion of the mother as a dominant figure, a strange version of ourselves we cannot help but feel ambivalence towards.

I did not recognise myself in these representations. I was already very aware of the ways in which I was like my own mother. Like her, I struggled to hold my tongue. Over the four decades I have been alive, I have fought with her as many times as I have reflected on what a gift it is to have a mother who values her own mind and thoughts so much that she knows they have to matter to the world. I do not always want to know what my mother thinks about my life choices. Yet, I am grateful that I was raised by her. I now recognise the value in many decisions my parents made about how to bring us up.

The daughter of a teacher and a woman who crossed a national border to marry the man she wanted, my mother is a consummate traveller and fluent in every language she speaks – a trait that she shared with all of her siblings. As a child, she was attentive to my most mundane preoccupations and always had a life of her own. Passionate about her career as a nurse, she often travelled away from home to study a course in a different city for weeks or months. I only distinctly recall stints in East London, Port Elizabeth and Pietermaritzburg, although there may have been more. Later, as an adult when she spent a few years on another continent for the same career, it seemed consistent with how she had always lived her life.

I learnt two things as I watched her passion for life, family and career: that a woman's dreams and pursuits matter and that a lifelong partnership allows such ambition. She also taught me that a man worth building a family with supported his partner's interests as passionately as he enjoyed his own. Even when she suddenly decided to register and graduate with two degrees in order to pursue a career in teaching, we adapted to enable this direction. My closest childhood friend's mother – married to my father's best friend since undergraduate days at Fort Hare – had been a psychiatric nurse when we were small but had retrained as a biology teacher, and worked until retirement in this new profession. My closest school-friend's parents lived and worked in towns a hundred kilometres apart. They are still married. I thought this was a normal expectation from heterosexual relationships well into my adulthood, and one I could take for granted. And, although I have since discovered – sometimes with horror and other times with devastation – that this is not a reality I can take for granted as available to those who want it, it is not one I am willing to accept life partnership without. I do not know how to try and learn how to be a self-sacrificing partner.

As much as I admire my mother and adored her for most of my childhood – save for a few years when I raged against her – it is a complicated relationship. She sets a very high bar for everything in my life. I constantly fall short of this bar, and she is mostly generous about my failures, and exceedingly proud of even my smallest accomplishments.

The relationship between a mother and daughter is a difficult one as we both get older. As I watch her become more delicate and age, I have felt resentment as she forcefully expressed her feelings. Yet, she has always done this, so it is my response that has changed. For a few years I thought my resentment stemmed from feeling like I was not enough for her, which is hard because my parents' approval is the only one that really mattered, but I have realised that the creeping resentment stems from a much scarier place.

As she grows older, I am reminded that she is human. Human beings become more fragile as they age. Because love between children and parents is sometimes a power tussle, I do not always know what to do with the fact that she needs me differently. Watching my father die and my mother age has changed me in ways I continue to resist. My Nkgono, my mother's mother, used to joke about how old people and babies are not just both close to heaven, but they are close to each other too. This makes more sense now than ever.

And so, as I watch my mother getting old, and less able to take care of herself, I am angered by the knowledge that she may soon not be able to take care of herself at all. What I know about this as natural and inevitable does little to temper my resentment. I realise now that I do not resent her for getting old. I am resentful *for* her. Dependence is the thing my mother finds most oppressive in the world. She is incurably independent. And I am my mother's daughter. I distinctly remember fighting with God as my Daddy's body succumbed to cancer and he grew dependent. Fiercely independent his whole life, I was furious that this was the way he was forced to die. I imagined his sharp mind at sixty-eight, trapped inside a body that was failing him.

I consider being able to take care of my mother a blessing. My parents took such good care of me, it is an honour to be able to. Except that it is difficult work to figure out how to only offer what is needed, and to communicate that my impatience is not towards her. At 44, I have a nine-year-old son, and my mind races to how young he will still be when I get old.

Perhaps none of this is special. Perhaps this is what people mean when they articulate a fear of ageing. I always imagined that I would age like Tina Turner, that I would wear bright-coloured lipstick, dangerously high heels and drink Chardonnay with breakfast in my 70s. I planned the perfect ageing that wasn't ageing at all. I have never been as fit as Tina Turner, so it was a fantasy. Alcohol has so long ceased to be a part of my life that I am amazed at the person I was when I imagined a free old age that included dry white wine as daily decadence. Watching my beautiful, independent, vibrant mother – who drives, shops and reads entire novels in bed now – feel less stable on her feet, shows me that ageing may be a gift but we do not get to plan it.

When I was in primary school, I worshipped my mother. I watched her every move, and I sat inside her wardrobe surrounded by her smell on her clothes when she was gone and I missed her. I cannot imagine a day when she is no longer here. I used to feel the same way about my father's mortality, and I am surviving his death one day at a time a decade later. My mother's fragility reminds me that such a day is nearing. In reality, she is not frail at all. She just does not have the body of a forty-year-old. She is not supposed to.

The idea of turning into her does not scare me. There have been moments when I have heard her words come out of my mouth as I talked to my children, so we are long past that point. Since I genuinely like my mother almost all of the time, I can live with that. I know that in both the ways I am like her, and in the ways that I am deliberately unlike her, I am always fully my mother's daughter. I annoy my sons as much as she sometimes frustrates me:

Vuyani tries to hide it behind a very specific laugh and shake of his head while Yethu does not try to hide it at all. Mothers are people too. We are not made to please our children. And children are not made to please us. These real lessons are much bigger and even harder to learn. Impatient daughters-turned-mothers sometimes make the worst students in this regard. I inherited my father's impatience but envy my mother's patience, instead.

While I am very clear about why I was parented well, I often battle to know with certainty when and if I am parenting well. I welcome this battle because I want children who are decent, generous, principled human beings committed to justice. It is important to me to parent well. And I derive untold daily pleasure from parenting. Everybody seems to think their children are wonderful, but mine truly are remarkable. I do not want them to be conventional men. Therefore I constantly reflect about what it means to parent well as a feminist. Feminist parenting is political, deliberate and non-negotiable for me. It is also slippery ground. That I have around me several beloved friends, committed to feminist parenting too, to observe and disagree with, helps.

However, we are different human beings and so I imagine that feminist parenting is not something that can ever have a manual. For me, it means trying to teach my children principles for living that are about valuing people regardless of what they look or identify as, knowing the value of their own voices and being able to live with integrity. It is never easy, but it is worth pursing this ability to live with oneself. Like the feminist mothers who took part in Fiona Joy Green's ten-year study, the work of feminist mothering is in the details for me. Green notes that

> [t]hrough contesting notions of motherhood and practices of mothering, by engaging in honest and sometimes challenging relationships with their children, as well as raising children to be critical thinkers who are able to articulate and challenge perspectives that do not necessarily confer with the status quo, feminist mothers believe they are continuing, and reaping the benefits of, the political activist work they began a decade or more

ago as mothers. They believe, with the support and assistance of feminists, the feminist work of mothering can be successfully done.

As a feminist who has chosen to parent, I frequently struggle with notions of mothering and motherhood specifically, and parenting more broadly that circulate and assume a taken-for-granted commonsensical status. Although I was spanked, I do not believe in using violence against those who have less structural power than me, and so there is no room for physical punishment in our home. However, whereas I can be the most imaginative person when it comes to how to live my life, punishment has been a constant challenge because I also battle with the line between disciplining and punishing.

For many years I found mothering to be both extremely rewarding and extremely isolating in many ways. The hostility to parenting comes mostly in the area of work. Life experiences change what enters our line of vision and what shade things take on. Parenting is no different. When Yethu was a toddler, the university I worked at first moved the childcare facility and preschool off campus to a different part of town, and then closed it altogether. A year later, there were campus-wide emails sent by the administration, admonishing parents who brought their children to work during university term time that coincided with school holidays.

I know what a significant time difference it made for my then partner and I to navigate the moving preschool once we had decided to keep him at the now private facility for his stability. I was parenting solo when that email made the rounds, and although I was not the target audience, since I rarely take my child to work with me, I was outraged. An institution which had closed its on-campus preschool, in a country where research shows most children live with a single parent, usually a mother, was shaming parents for difficult parenting choices. Taking a child to work is not a decision most parents take lightly because it is exceedingly hard to work with your child present. It requires more than the daily juggling, but the impossible task of simultaneously, minute-by-minute, doing two jobs at once all day.

This is what well-intentioned gender progressives who routinely suggest "bringing" a small child along to workshops, seminars and conferences to counter a parent's stated inability to attend fail to grasp. I have been the feminist who suggested this too in my pre-parenting days, so I fully appreciate the sentiment from both directions.

People mean well, and they do well. My feminist parenting friends constantly challenge me to know and do better all the time, but there are moments that are permanently tattooed on my memory. Upon return from an extended trip during which her husband, Ali, had become temporary single parent so that she could dedicate uninterrupted time to her doctoral thesis, Nthabiseng Motsemme was met with constant commentary on how wonderful her husband is. I am not disputing this. Her response, however, was both necessary and illuminating.

She pointed out that parenting is always hard work that needed to be done well, that theirs were as much hers as they were her husband's children. She meant this at the level of responsibility. Therefore, she cautioned against praising him for being a good father for doing what is taken for granted when mothers do it. She was not questioning how good a father he was. She was reminding all of us that we normalise good, full-time parenting by treating it as normal.

I recently had to repeat Nthabiseng's words to a friend whose partner has a child with someone from a previous relationship. She had been generally praising her new partner as a wonderful person, and as she listed his attributes, had pointed to how much regular time he made for his teenage son, and what an attentive father he was. I said, "as he should". When I first met her, two decades ago, both her parents were still alive and married to each other. She had grown up with the attention of both. So, I found the rendering of proper parenting as exceptional when performed by her new partner curious. She pointed that I was right that he should, but his choices were praiseworthy because they were not the norm.

It struck me that this was precisely where the problem lay: that when men perform childrearing with full-attention, in the way we demand of women, we heap extra praise on them. This is what

Nthabiseng was pointing to as dangerous patriarchal work for those of us who claim feminist politics.

All of us retain aspects of our own upbringing in the parenting choices we make. A recent conversation with one of my best friends, Thulani, about his son's sudden refusal to kiss and/or hug close family friends caused some disruption. He is like my brother. His children call me the forms of aunt that designate "father's sister" in two different languages, and my younger son calls him malume. He was particularly concerned when his elder son would not hug me goodbye. His anxieties about how to reinforce a sustained, routine, respectful language of affection collided with my anxieties about teaching children to be comfortable to reject adults touching them. Where my friend was alarmed, I was pleased by my nephew's ability to assert boundaries about his own body. As we chatted, and because we have listened to each other for more than half our lives, we both sat with a view that is very different from our own. There is constant value for me in this. Indeed, this is one of the greatest gifts of chosen family.

However, very few idioms grate me more than "it takes a village", living as I do where most children are raised by a single parent. It seems a misguided, out of touch statement, that also invisibilises the enormous work required for single or dual parenting. It is not that we need acknowledgement as single mothers and fathers, or coupled-up parents. It is simply irritation at the negation of such work.

In her repeated interviews with a group of feminist mothers over a period of ten years, Fiona Joy Green finds that the mothers agree on various aspects of their parenting. These pertain not only to the experience of mothering in deliberately political ways, but also to the valuation and interruption of mothering in wider society. For example, she writes,

> [n]ot only are there social pressures on "good mothers" ... who are expected to be doing "it all," feminist mothers experience additional expectations or pressure to be competent and capable women from feminists who don't have children.

The pressure to perform as though I did not have a baby, and later toddler, in my house almost drove me insane. When overburdened colleagues would insist that they cope because of how much work they do at home daily, I would almost break down in tears – not in front of them, but later on my own. The workloads were unrealistic, but I had also done a significant amount of work at home when I did not have a small child. My own frustration with diminished work capacity as a mother with a baby rhymed with these statements, and both were exacerbated by the fact of being the most senior – and only Black woman professor – in my school. Although I knew all the counter-arguments against the trap of the strong Blackwoman, and against the burden of representation that minoritised people carry, I was not free of the mixture of shame and disappointment in myself. The academy makes demands as though professors have adult children, no children, or a wife responsible for the bulk of the parenting. A breastfeeding, sleep-deprived professor is almost impossible to imagine, and more than once told of how much more productive her older male professor colleagues were when their children were smaller.

Still, in all the ways that really count – even when I am gossiping about her with my sisters, or teasing her with my brother – I am absolutely my mother's daughter.

In her deceptively short memoir, *Alone,* Lebo Pule reflects on the many challenges of taking mothering seriously as a feminist. She does so in a variety of ways. In one instance, after the failure of her first business, she decides to move back home with her children and allow her hardworking mother to help them, while she hands over her third child, Tau, at six months, to his father for primary caretaking in order to figure out how to get back on her feet.

Although she knows she needs help, and that children are the responsibility of more than one person, she battles with feelings of guilt and inadequacy as a mother who is unable to take care of her children in accordance with her own desire and designs. She is pained by how much help she needs, even if temporarily.

Pule writes

> I slipped into a mini depression. I couldn't think, I couldn't eat, but I slept. I slept for hours on end and was negligent of the children, it was easier with the bigger children, Tsholo and Thebe. They were fifteen and nine respectively but I was not coping with Tau, who was six months old at the time. I made another hard decision, the hardest decision a mother could ever take; I arranged with Tau's father to help me with him. I asked him to take the baby for a while, for a few months until I had re-established my life. I needed to focus on getting a job. Tau needed fulltime attention and energy. My mother was a great help but she worked a full day. She needed to, her daughter had come back home with all her children. I will always be grateful to Tau's father and grandmother, who looked after Tau for nearly a year while I was getting myself on track. Though the relief was great, the guilt gnawed at me. I fetched him every weekend without fail, getting so impatient on my way to pick him up on Friday afternoons, as the traffic to Midrand was unbearable. My heart would break every Sunday evening when we had to part.
>
> I never liked the idea of separating children, but I needed to take that decision. We were all overwhelmed, including my parents.

Although Pule makes the correct decisions, she is almost paralysed by guilt. This undeserved guilt is still there, later, as she makes amends to her children thus:

> I gathered my children around and apologized for what I had put them through. I promised them that I was working very hard to make sure that this situation does not happen again. I would never unnecessarily put my needs first before theirs.

I recognised so much in her feelings, and was utterly delighted to read about her mother's response. Pule's mother's attitude to mothering is very different to her own:

> [w]hen I stopped at my mother's home in Alexandra to see the children, I would take between five and ten minutes to speak to her

alone. I would thank her for looking after my children, for both mothering and grandmothering them. She always found those gratitude moments strange, she did not understand where I was coming from. After all, she was the grandmother and did what she had to do. I knew she did not have to take on my responsibility. This is where the generation gap came in. My mother saw a need; she could help and she did. She never considered the modern way of thinking; letting children suffer just because someone had made a blunder and a mess of their life. It was important that I acknowledge the role she was playing in my and my children's lives.

When you take parenting seriously, you do not take the labour of those who parent your children with you for granted. I have written about my own gratitude in an earlier chapter of this book.

I look forward to parenting differently for the rest of my life – less actively when they are both adult men. I also know that Sithabile Ndlovu, the woman who has been a part of mine and Yethu's life since he was two months old, has made things possible in my life that I could not have done without her. Although she is an employee, rather than a family member, her labour has enabled me to keep a vibrant career and the satisfaction I derive from that while enjoying parenting.

CHAPTER 13

After Sobukwe
Time again for Africa's imagination

I was deeply honoured by the invitation to present the Public Lecture hosted by the Steve Biko Foundation, the Robert Mangaliso Sobukwe Trust, and the University of Fort Hare, in memory of one of the biggest visionaries we have ever had. I am a Fort Hare baby, so it is always wonderful to come to work in anything Fort Hare related. Both my parents and two of my siblings graduated from the University of Fort Hare. I also grew up on the East Campus of Fort Hare's Alice campus and my father taught Organic Chemistry at that Institution until he retired. It is clear to me that being raised in the Fort Hare of the '70s and '80s has much to do with what I grew up to take for granted about African genius, African intellectual life, African creativity and entitlement to excellence, espoused by Africans from different parts of East, West and Southern Africa who were academics and students on that campus, as I played, unaware of first Biko's death a few months before and then Sobukwe's death a few days before I started Sub A. The vision of myself – for a Blackgirl in apartheid South Africa, an African child in the shadow of the African torment of slavery, colonialism, genocide and apartheid – is a debt I cannot repay to Fort Hare, but it is one that I hope to have repaid by the time I leave this dimension of earth.

Let me start again.

As I share my thoughts and provocations tonight, I want to conjure up an image of Mangaliso Sobukwe that is slightly out of focus in post-apartheid Southern Africa. We concentrate usually on the man who gave us the Pan Africanist Congress in 1959, the man who was imprisoned in 1960 on Robben Island, the revolutionary whose vision, words, humaneness is known to everybody who is here today. I want to talk about Sobukwe's valuing of the imagination, evoke the Sobukwe who took great pleasure in the non-obvious, who was creative in as much as he relished the works of the imagination. But he also understood the value of the imagination when unbounded, not limited to the pages of a novel or a performance on stage. That is what the iconic image of Sobukwe letting soil fall through his fingers is: recourse to the metaphoric, the poetic, and the symbolic, when ordinary words were both unavailable and inadequate. This image is iconic, even as invisibilised as Sobukwe is, it is a moment we recognise from how we speak about him. Although he lived in brutal times, he spoke in his inaugural speech in 1959 of "living in an era that is pregnant with untold possibilities for both good and evil" – a time of confusion, brutality, closing in, but a time that also offered possibilities for imagining new pathways to freedom.

To keep him company I want to conjure up other Pan Africanists who inspired as much as they discomfited.

The late great Kofi Awonoor ends one of his best known poems, much loved by literary Pan Africanists of all ages, 'The Weaverbird', with the following lines:

We look for new homes every day
For new altars we strive to rebuild
The old shrines defiled from the weaver's excrement (ll. 14–16)

Here, Awonoor invites us to reimagine ourselves anew after colonial conquest, rather than hanker after a return to a past that is impossible to reach again. Notably, his is an optimistic view: although the search for homes is ongoing, it is possible to achieve: home is possible again. An Africa in which we can take stock of what we have lost, but in which we remain unwavering in our commitment to finding new ways of honouring ourselves again as African, expanding freedoms, doing the difficult work of love and freedom, being unafraid of asking questions that seem counter-intuitive.

The second defiant, freedom-loving Pan Africanist I want to conjure up is Wambui Otieno, Mau Mau scout, feminist, impossible to contain; a woman who defied expectations of class, marriage, love and geography. Running away from her late colonial middle-class family to join Mau Mau as a scout and fighter broke both gender and class expectations at the time. A highly efficient guerrilla, she was sold out by her comrade and fiancé and raped by a colonial soldier while in detention. She laid a charge against him, even though she knew that the odds of her word being taken seriously in a colonial court was minimal. Wambui Otieno formed part of a parliament in an independent Kenya and left when she no longer agreed with some of her comrades ideologically. She went on to build the largest law firm in independent Kenya with her new husband and, when he died, unsuccessfully sued his family in order to bury him where he wanted to be, rather than the ancestral land the family deemed fit. Many years later, she fell in love with and married a man who was to be her lover until her death: working class who was also a third her age. A more inappropriate match seemed hard to imagine for large swathes of the Kenyan public.

Sitting and listening to aspects of her life in 2014, Wambui Otieno sounds like she lived an adventurous life. Yet, this is only possible if we allow ourselves to forget that this was a woman who lived in a colonised land, fought to free her land, made choices that required nothing short of audacity for an African girl and woman. She lived a life with such brazen capacity for the imagination that she makes many of our twenty-first-century lives in a democracy appear quite tame. Her life showed such determined capacity to pursue her principles and desires that external censure could not contain her.

I think these three, Sobukwe, Awonoor and Otieno, would sit well together.

But what do I want them to do? I want them to help us ask some strange questions about our Africa today and many of the things that frighten, frustrate and threaten to tear us further down. I thought it important to start from a position of hope before I try to make sense of what it might mean to think about African unity in Sobukwe's terms, to think of ours as an age, ourselves in 2014 as "living in an era that is pregnant with untold possibilities for good and evil" – a time of confusion, brutality, closing in, but a time that also offers possibilities for imagining new pathways to freedom.

Boko Haram has slaughtered thousands of people in Nigeria over the last five years or so. They hit brutally and with regularity. And Borno has suffered more than its fair share of violence from this group. The Nigerian state's army and resources appear ill-equipped to deal with the onslaught. In recent days there have been renewed suggestions that Boko Haram was funded from within President Goodluck Jonathan's government. Such insinuations deepen the mystery that is Boko Haram for many of us inside and outside Nigeria who encounter them primarily through news coverage.

One thing is clear, though: the disjuncture between how we speak about Boko Haram's reign of terror. We focus on their fundamentalist Muslim identity. We wonder about the strangeness of illogically motivated kidnappings of girls. We turn away from the kinds of slaughter that Africans subject one another to. We deal with them one at a time, imagining we can bring our girls home without facing the reality of who/what Boko Haram is, of how and why Boko Haram exists.

Boko Haram clearly sees the abduction of girls as linked to earlier kidnappings, shooting and bombing sprees. Their reign of terror has long targeted schools, government buildings and police stations. They also hit mainly economically and geographically marginalised communities, but not exclusively. They have abducted boys before.

It is all part of the same project for them. We may have a better chance of unravelling the mysteries, seeing through the smoke and mirrors if we, too, pay attention to the patterns, rather than to individual parts of the Boko Haram phenomenon as though delinked.

Calling them terrorists and cries that we are losing the war on terror is laziness. The war on terror is something very specific and I am pretty certain it is not a war that is meant to see Africans win anything. It is not a framework with the African world in mind or heart. In fact, it is an imperialist project that Africans continue to pay in blood and land for.

What happens when we read Boko Haram as something distinct from, but also similar to Al Shabaab, whose bombings and abductions in Kenya were catapulted into global awareness during the Westgate Mall attack? That is when Kofi Awonoor, whose poem I read earlier, was killed. Where he is, the symbolism of the Al Shabaab killing such a visible Pan Africanist who was in Nairobi for a literature festival is not lost on him.

But Boko Haram is not Al Shabaab. Their transitioning into public consciousness was very different. I had been struck by how strangely militarised Nairobi was the week before the Nairobi attacks. Kenyan friends and colleagues noted that the presence of heavily armed soldiers outside buildings in the city, the individual body searches as we tried to enter and leave various buildings had something to do with US presence and how it dictated what safe cities looked like. You will remember that there were many more Kenyan casualties to the 1998 bombings of the US embassy in Nairobi than US citizens.

In this heavily militarised Nairobi, Al Shabaab struck a mall frequented by the elite, expatriates, and European tourists. And this was the first time many people had heard about Al Shabaab, as we watched a series of mystifications, counter-accusations and conspiracy theories on what was happening.

It is easy to say Boko Haram targets poor girls and Al Shabaab targets the wealthy and powerful, and that therefore they have nothing in common. They are not part of the same phenomenon. But what happens if we assume that reading them alongside and through each other can teach us something otherwise occluded when we pay attention only to singular events by such groups, disconnected from other dimensions of their activities?

Lest you imagine that what I am bothered by in Al Shabaab and Boko Haram has to do with groups of bandits, or Muslim militias, let me throw more examples in the mix. I am talking specifically about two pieces of legislation whose levels of violence contribute similarly to what Boko Haram and Al Shabaab are engaged in: The Same Sex Marriage Prohibition Act of 2014, signed in by President Goodluck Jonathan in January 2014 and the Ugandan Anti-Homosexuality Act of 2014. The latter was so hastily put through that it was challenged by an unprecedented number of petitioners in March 2014 under the Civil Society Coalition on Human Rights and Constitutional Law. These petitioners noted everything from how such legislation was in direct contravention of the Ugandan Constitution, how it was unprocedurally passed through with minimal parliamentary support, in sittings that were not quorate, as well as slating it for the violence it authorised against those who live in Uganda. This Bill had been part of our consciousness for a while because it had been previously successfully pushed back before its hurried passing in January 2014.

Nigeria's Same Sex Prohibition Act may be less familiar to us. On 15 January 2014, a statement by the Nigerian Lesbian, Gay, Bisexual, Transgender, Intersex in Diaspora noted not only the dismay at the passing of such a law, but also noted that such legislation "gives official validation to the harassment of sexual minorities ... [and] provide[s] a cover for unscrupulous individuals and state institutions including the police to hunt down, intimidate and harass citizens based on their actual or suspected sexual orientation".

It is not hard to see how they get to this conclusion, given that the law allows, among other things, fourteen-year jail sentences for same-sex marriage, ten years for displays of affection between people of the same gender, a ten-year jail term for anyone who enables or associates with people in same-sex marriage or relationship, as well as a ten-year jail sentence that would only apply to LGBTI rights activists. It not only terrorises and delegitimises desire and affection, it also turns ordinary citizens into agents of this terror regime. So, in order to avoid imprisonment for having queer family or friends, you have to turn them in, disown them or otherwise distance yourself from them.

Inside the country, Initiative for Equality (Ife) spends enormous resources and time, at great risk to debunk many of the fallacies at the heart of such laws: that they are unAfrican, that nowhere before in African history have people fallen in love and/or desired each other within the same gender and sex, as well as showing the way in which such a law terrorised not only "sexual minorities" but the large numbers of Nigerians who support same-sex marriage.

What these acts of brutality – whether by supposedly mysterious groupings or with state sanction – achieve is fairly similar. Jessica Horn notes that

> [t]he gender dynamics of the Chibok crisis signals a worrying trend across the African continent, as religious fundamentalist views take hold and find their place not just in fringe extremists, but in capturing policies and actions of the state, and perhaps more worryingly, the popular imagination.

You will all be aware of the very vocal Christian right in defending homophobic laws in Uganda, Nigeria but also closer to home. There is no contradiction between this and claiming that same-sex desire, diverse gender expression and desire for autonomy are un-African. Kopano Ratele's scholarship shows us how easily conservative bodies within and outside African state bodies marshal fossilised "African culture", "sharia law", or "the Bible" to close down avenues for African freedom, imagination and diversity. Although Islam gets its fair share of blame fundamentalisms that are epistemically and physically violent, Jessica Horn reminds us again that when talking about the rise of contemporary structures of violence, fundamentalist Christianity needs to remain in our analytical frame. Legislation controlling women's dress under the Anti-Pornography Act in Uganda and the failed Indecent Dressing Bill in Nigeria were both developed in the name of highly conservative expressions of Christian morality, and alongside the much critiqued legislation in both countries expanding anti-gay laws and the criminalization of same-gender sexual acts and advocacy for equality.

Where Horn says religion, we could just as easily substitute "culturalist arguments", for her Anti-Pornography Act/Indecent Dressing Bill, we could transplant "Traditional Courts Bill". And we may have impeccable legislation in South Africa, but that is not always much consolation when dealing with lynched, decapitated gay men in the Northern Cape or the broken bodies of lesbians in the Western Cape. It is not Muslim fundamentalists who are stripping young women in various Southern African countries for wearing short skirts, trousers or not fitting into tidy notions of appropriate sex, gender expression or identity. But the effects are remarkably similar – living with the constant awareness that you can be arrested, attacked or bombed (depending on which part of the continent you live in) for living truthfully, pursuing freedom is living in a state of terror. It is constant communication that you do not matter. The danger is real whether the state you pay taxes to threatens to throw you in jail for being an activist, for falling in love, or for wanting to go to school as a girl.

Sobukwe, Awonoor and Otieno reminded us again and again that Africa's fate is intertwined. They dedicated their lives to intertwined freedoms, joys and imagination. Sobukwe spoke, even as a student, of the principle of a single Africa: that this interconnectedness could easily translate into the untold possibilities for harm. As attentive as we are to possibilities for unity, renaissance, renewal and restoration of Africa to itself, Sobukwe's invitation is to keep our eye on patterns that pull us in the opposite direction; that seek to enslave us again.

The closing down of routes to full African human expression that I have outlined through militia, state and other fundamentalist expression on our continent are not part of Sobukwe's united Africa. They are a violent expression of the "untold possibilities for evil", to use again and again Sobukwe's words. Whether the rise of wealthy and violent Christian and Muslim fundamentalisms on our continent is as directly funded by right-wing United States and right-wing Saudi Arabian interest – as a significant amount of scholarship and thinking from our continent now suggests – or whether these oppressive regimes of terror are more complicated in source, one thing is clear: expanding the reign of terror for African people – through guns, legislation, fear of broken bodies – is the kind of African unity we would do well without.

All of these expressions of violence – Boko Haram, Al Shabaab, legislation that criminalises love, friendship and imagination – create a realm of terror and of control. They narrow the range of what is possible. Whether they say the Q'uran forbids it, the Bible punishes it, or no African has ever been like you before, they are hateful. They say there is only one way to be African and all other forms will be obliterated. No amount of force and mystification is too much for this kind of genocide.

Writing in the "lost chapter" from his memoir, *One day I will write about this*, Binyavanga Wainaina says:

> I am twenty nine. It is 11 July, 2000. I, Binyavanga Wainaina, quite honestly swear I have known I am a homosexual since I was five. I have never touched a man sexually. I have slept with three women in my life. One woman, successfully. Only once with her. It was amazing. But the next day, I was not able to.

Christian and Muslim fundamentalists say "you are immoral and no Allah/God made you, abomination. Your body must be torn apart". Their African traditionalist allies agree and add "you are unAfrican. No African before you has ever had this desire. You must be stopped, silenced, tortured, jailed."

Chimamanda Ngozi Adichie says, rather than violence, it bodes us well to embrace humility and humanity. "There is humility in accepting that there are things we simply don't know", reminding us that African, human expression comes in all forms, not just in the ones we personally inhabit. Writing of her childhood friend Sokuchukwuma's awareness of his difference at eight, like Wainaina who knew at five, she continues:

> It was not about sex, because it could not have been – his hormones were of course not yet fully formed – but it was an awareness of himself, and other children's awareness of him, as different. He could not have 'chosen the lifestyle' because he was too young to do so. And why would he – or anybody – choose to be homosexual in a world that makes it so hard for homosexuals?

Sobukwe says, "[w]e are what we are because the God of Africa made us so. We dare not compromise, nor dare we use moderate language in the course of our freedom."

Wambui Otieno's life inspired us to pursue freer ways of being, whether these be for schooling for girls in areas where Boko Haram deems it inappropriate or living with integrity in areas where some South Africans think it is unacceptable to be a man who loves men. She reminds us that the imagination and desire have an intimate relationship with freedom. Kofi Awonoor invites us not to pretend our pre-colonial pasts were prisons lacking imagination. Instead, he challenges us to strive for an Africa where freedom and imagination reign. Sobukwe spoke of being limited in where you can move (he was speaking of passes not of "curative/corrective" rape, Traditional Courts, Boko Haram or Al Shabaab, but he may as well have been) is like carrying again the badge of slavery. Every revolutionary we love as Pan Africanists says along with Che Guevara that all injustice is connected.

All violence, as I have discussed here, whether it limits movement or silences self-expression, narrows the range of what is possible. The use of the threat of violence to kill autonomy is an old oppressive tactic. We can continue to treat each situation as separate and allow ourselves to be confused even as we feel in very concrete terms the erosion of hard-won freedoms everywhere on the continent, until all African women are again silent children as we were under colonising regimes. We can pretend that the onslaught is in our imagination. Many of us grew up with boys and men that held hands as friends and/or as lovers. If I remember this clearly and Adichie raised in a different part of the continent remembers it too, many of you do too.

When did we become people who consider affection so threatening?

When did Africans, who have been various kinds of Christians and Muslims for many centuries, find it impossible to live with difference?

When did this become the African way?

Accepting that being docile, disowning our variety and versions of ourselves that gave us joy in the past is what being African is today is doing missionary work on ourselves. It is being complicit to being rendered terrorists, and agreeing to terrorise others until they, too, are metaphorically exiled.

Here is prophetic Sobukwe's vision again, speaking in 1949 at Fort Hare:

> This is a difficult period to analyse. It is a confused period, such as only Mqhayi, Bereng or Dickens could describe. We are witnessing today the disintegration of old empires, and the integration of old communities. [...] But this time the imperialism we see is not the naked brutal mercantile imperialism of the 17th and 18th centuries. It is a more subtle one.

Later in the same speech, he says, more hopefully:

> Let me plead with you, lovers of my Africa, to carry with you into the world the vision of a new Africa, an Africa reborn, an Africa rejuvenated, an Africa recreated, young AFRICA. We are the first glimmers of a new dawn. And if we are persecuted for our views, we should remember, as the African saying goes, that it is darkest before dawn, and that the dying beast kicks most violently when it is giving up the ghost, so to speak.

What does it mean to use intellectual and creative wealth in defence of ourselves, as Sobukwe invites us to in 1959? The man in whose name we are gathered today challenged us not to look away from the difficult. A difficult period requires imagination. He mentions three imaginative figures: Mqhayi, Bereng, Dickens. Sobukwe, the lover of literature, of the imagination as central to the work of freedom – not as entertainment, escape, distraction. The responsibility that comes with the enormous gift of living after Sobukwe is that we must ask even those questions that we have no answers to yet so that we may imagine the range of possibilities, question ourselves even when it hurts, and question our own comrades like Nomfanelo Kota, Wambui Otieno and Pregs Govender did and do, when things seem amiss. Honest appraisal of Africa, African inheritance; and I am sure if Sobukwe were physically alive today he would also insist that we question what "African" is used to mean when it leads to the obliteration of African life, the trivialisation of African joy, the bombing of African affection.

Africa has to mean a present and future home again for those who strive for a freedom linked to the freedom of those like – and unlike – us. Michael Eric Dyson insists that for those of us who are children of the African world (and maybe for others),

> [h]ome is the geography of the imagination. For me, it's also about the architecture of identity through aspiration and yearning, since home is carved from hope and memory. It is both forward-looking and backward leaning. [...] Like identity, home, to a large degree, is composed of an evolving awareness about how you can decrease the discomfort you have in the world as a result of your roots.

Home is an optimistic claim, then, aspiration attentive to the past and desirous of a free future. It is an engagement with the mess that is also part of our inheritance. Jessica Horn argues that

> [i]t requires persistent public reaffirmation of critical thinking and debate [...] strengthening progressive social movements, and the

bravery to stand up in defense of the marginalized in our society. It also requires that we are more assertive in our defense of women's rights.

And I add, the rights of others, even when we are not the ones being rendered homeless. It requires rejecting solutions to the threat of Al Shabaab terror like the marshalling of Somalis into refugee camps such as we now see in Kasarani camps in Kenya, about which Grace A Musila has said "[t]hese faces and images remind me of photographs of camps where suspected Mau Mau were held by the British administration in colonial Kenya". An independent democratic Kenyan government is responsible for this image.

It is darkest before dawn, Sobukwe says. But only if we fight for the morning rising of the sun, he adds. Like Binyavanga Wainaina, "I am a Pan Africanist. I belong to this continent."

Like him, I also recognise that all of the hateful legislation and political manoeuvring is a way to deflect from other political matters. It seems both of us, like many other people on the continent, find enormous value, and along with Sobukwe share "the principle that Africa is one and desires to be one [....] We can never do enough for Africa, nor can we love her enough. The more we do for her, the more we wish to do."

I am not as sure as Sobukwe that Africa is a she. But I am sure that it is home, a home worth defending as part of honouring him, ourselves, a home worth restoring to freedom of all Africa's children.

It is a huge task. I hold on to his optimism because my own is shaky right now. Sobukwe says "Africa will be free …. She will be heard." And this desire to be free is because "[w]e are what we are because the God of Africa made us so. We dare not compromise, nor dare we use moderate language in the course of our freedom."

CHAPTER 14

A love letter to the Blackman who fathered me

Dear Daddy,
One of my earliest coherent memories is of you looking across to Mamam when I stood left hand on our old coffee table, quite pleased with having repeated after the University of Fort Hare students who said it all the time as they ran around, "Black Power"! I don't know how old I was, but I know it was before I went to school, so it must have been between my birth in the last month of 1972 and my first school year in 1978. I remember Mamam looked back at you and threw her head back laughing. I remember her light coloured slip dress, and both your pleased responses, and your words: "Uthini, sisi?" I know you continue to call all three of your daughters, us, "sisi", whose intimacy and affection is so difficult to translate into the English "sister", or even "big sister" literally. I guess it is closer in translation meaningfully to what Mamam calls all of us individually: "my baby", in addition to the slew of nicknames she bestows on all of us.

As an adult who knows how powerful that slogan was, and

understands more every day, about why it needed to, and needs to mean so much, I am struck by what it must have given my young Blackchild-self to grow up hearing it every day for a while, even if I did not know what it meant. I realise that when I said it, Bantu Biko must have still been alive. This would be one of the joys of being born and brought up in the early seventies. To be able to know that Black and power could dance together, and not have to teach myself to believe it as young men and women of your generations must have had to in the third decade of apartheid. But what does all this mean about being here in 2004, ten years into our freedom? Being here is wondering whether what the Palestinian revolutionary, Edward Said, suggested about ideas and theories travelling can be thought through in relation to identities. Am I a different Black South African than I would have been had I been born and raised at another time, in another home? What does this mean in 2004? It is not inconceivable that Blackness, being Black, or this meaning of being South African I carry within me, travels paradoxically. After all, look at the many different things it comes to mean at home – legally, politically, socially, regionally, seriously, playfully, frighteningly, reassuringly, effectively, powerfully, historically and surprisingly. We become who we are because of who raises us.

I also remember bawling, holding onto your leg and sitting on your foot as you tried to go to work. I remember that once you actually let me come along to your Organic Chemistry lecture, that you said something about your daughter sitting at the front of the class. I am amused now by how I battled to redraw diagrams resonant of the atomic and molecular structures I'd seen you lay out for your students. I imagine that somehow indulging what they must have read as your incredibly precocious child, even though this feels like it happened only on one day, your students and you somehow made me feel that a lecture hall is a place that I belong to if that is a belonging I choose. I wonder how much that has to do with my love of teaching and my choice of tertiary teaching and research, over the last decade, as my calling and first adult love. I am certain it has much to do with my conviction that knowledge is my entitlement, and one I can reach out for and work for as desired. More knowledgeable about the place of racism in the world, I am aware of the enormous symbolism of growing up in a university town where so many of the academic staff, and all of the students were Black. To see myself reflected in the world in such diversity: male and female, South African, Namibian, Ghanaian, Ugandan, Swazi, I thought that was how the world worked. I witnessed Black dance with Power, and Pride and Beauty every day.

I was in such a hurry to learn to read that I can almost taste the feeling of that day, in mid-1978, lying in bed between Mamam and you because I'd insisted, and my sisters had decided on other preoccupations for an early Sunday morning post-Mass, and showing you both that I could read. I remember Mamam lay half-changed from her Mass outfit, and you, still pyjama-d. I can imagine as an adult how long it must have taken to read the English-medium Sunday paper in my isiXhosa logic, for I'd just learnt how to read and didn't know how to read English yet. I remember being slightly puzzled that my recognition of the letters didn't always make sense. As an adult, I realise this must have taken a very long time because I remember taking my time and turning pages. I also remember how proud you and Mamam looked. The pleasure I/we (your children) can read off your faces is one of the reasons we all often come home to tell you even those things that could be told on the phone.

I know how powerful violent systems of knowledge are, how brutally successful they are in making us hate ourselves. In the face of this, that we could take so much for granted as Blackchildren, that I would surprise myself well into my twenties when I realised how much I took for granted – what I always assumed Black people could do – is testimony to the enormous power of assertions of hearing "Black Power" so many times as a child, and being raised by two people who could materially afford to raise us in accordance with that dance. I am not saying that I imagine you and Mamam sat down mid-engagement and carefully designed plans to raise us in the most concertedly well-structured out way. At the same time, how you raise your children is never an accident. I recognise that there are many Black men and women who could not have made these choices because materially, historically, the intrusion of what Achille Mbembe has called Africa's "chaotic nightmare" (which encompassed enslavement, colonisation, apartheid and neo-colonisation) affected them differently. I acknowledge that my benefits, my "taken-for-granted" areas, as well as those of my siblings, and some of our friends, have much to do with the material and academic access you made available. At the same time, I know that many village-educated and raised South Africans imbibed ways of self-love that were being threatened elsewhere.

Anyway, Daddy-wam-ndedwa qha, as I decided in a possessive fit of jealousy once as a child, as though claiming you as mine alone would un-Daddy you to my siblings, I know you know I love you. Children can't help loving their parents. But I would have chosen to love you, and being brought up by you anyway. Yes, I remember how cross I have been with you at times and all our fights when I was a teenager. But I love being your child, I adored it when I was a little girl, and I delight in it as an adult. I loved knowing that sitting on your lap was okay for as long as I could fit, that being with you felt safe and good. I liked trying to figure out why your hair seemed so much softer to the touch than mine and Mamam's, and later my brother's, why yours was so much closer to my sisters' texture. I love that you let us speak and engaged with my creative, political, feminist, crazy, romantic ideas for the three decades I have been alive. I love that even when I strongly disapproved of your personal choices, as I grew up, you inevitably communicated to me my choices and options in the kinds of Blackwomen and Blackmen I would allow into my life as partners and friends. It also meant that I would continue to be surprised by the often non-Black assumption that we define our realities, and community, primarily through our experiences of oppression. When there is so much pleasure, so many different points of connection and dissonance when I encounter other Black people, I know that I am hardly exceptional in this regard.

But, how did I get here by way of Biko and Said? It could be the same way little Jackie Kay, who was to grow into a phenomenal writer, could kiss an Angela Davis poster, the only person she'd seen whose skin tone matched herself living as she did in Scotland. When little Jackie hoped that the activist would feel the love inside the cold jail of another continent, did the temperature in the activist's cell rise for a split second? Perhaps. The wonder of paying attention to Black creativity being powerful is identical to Miriam Makeba re-defining music while making headlines in the US and coincidentally starting a hairstyle that grew synonymous with global Blackness when proud: the Afro. Or when Miriam Tlali walked into a shop in-between studying and not studying at a Jo'burg university, wrote an explosively beautiful novel about Muriel leaving some racist Metropolitan shop, and it was clear as day that danger was brewing. And before anybody knew it, there were people writing and calling themselves staffriders all over the place. I guess the thing about this roving sense of Blackness is that you never know where you will land, and when this complicated business of freedom is thrown in, surprises abound.

I appreciate and love that I can talk to you about work, politics, career and almost all sorts of things as an adult. Even when I censor some topics because intimacy does not mean all-access, I love that I have you as my Daddy. I know that not every girl-child has had that, and that even fewer adult women can access it. I value that you must have made a conscious choice to create that as a possibility for your now feminist daughters, and your self-reflexive son. I love you for all these things and so many others. I love you for making it possible for us to anger, disapprove of and hurt each other, as all families must, without that being the central definitive part of our relationship. I love that we talk so often on the phone, that you let me force you to celebrate your birthday and Father's Day. I delight in watching you recollect the strangest things about your children's early years, and get tickled by your grandchildren's peculiarities, knowing you are a constant in all our lives and aware of the difficult choices you've made about family. I am stunned that you can make sense of the difficult, and for me, often infuriating, responsibility you have taken on and continue to shoulder in relation to our larger family. I love, at the same time, that you have taught us about responsibility to family no matter what the cost: that family takes care of family and that at extremes boundaries have to be set. I know you know what I mean.

At the same time, I am grateful that you have taught me that relationships can be about joy, laughter and love. I am grateful that my soul chose you as the self-reflective Daddy to be fathered by, that so many of the things in Black Consciousness thought that I find so compelling are things you taught us, your children, to take for granted, that as I watch you age, you still continue, by the actions you live to teach, challenge and excite me.

And so, Daddy, in spite of our differences over the years, and due to our similarities, I thank you for the battles I did not have to fight in order to learn to love my Blackwoman self. I thank you for the contradictions and affirmations. I am grateful for the Blackman you are, were, chose to be, for the mistakes you probably wish I did not witness you make, and for all the work you did to make sure that for every minute I have been alive I would know that you would always love me unconditionally and that I mattered. I am proud of the Blackman you were and are and,

> I will always be your
> Gugu.

*postscript

My father and I wrote letters to each other regularly from my teens and later these would be emails until shortly before he died. When I was at boarding school at Inanda seminary outside Durban, from 1985 to 1987, he sent me a letter every week, and I replied every week. The first letter of each month came with cash, my pocket money, in a registered envelope. The other letters came in regular envelopes. The letters would temporarily cease when I changed schools to All Saints Senior College outside Bhisho in 1988 because I saw him every week, but they resumed when I moved to Cape Town to study at the University of Cape Town. At 14 or so, I started regularly telling my father that I loved him out loud and in writing. This letter has been revised only twice. It is an actual letter I wrote and gave to him one Father's Day in my late teens. I revised it in 2004 for possible publication as part of a collective project about Black love and imagination that never appeared in print. I showed him the revised version and let him know of my intention to publish it. He had kept the original version in the same file he kept my birth, Baptismal, First Holy Communion certificates; every letter I had ever written to him, and every single report card issued for me since Sub-A. He had such a file for each of his five children. I have not revised it again, and so retain the address mode, and the use of the present tense, even though my Daddy died a few days before Christmas in 2006. Four of his children called him Daddy for reasons that have never been clear to me since we all spoke to him in our mother tongue; and our half-brother referred to him more conventionally. All our letters were in English, and I suspect my obsessive re-reading of *UDike noCikizwa* as a child and adult came from my desperate attempts to fashion a written love language in my mother tongue.

Departures

When I was dreaming about my future writer life as a teenager, I imagined something more like the writers in television series. Each of my books so far has been written through a very different process, although there are similarities in when I am most likely to write or procrastinate and how many thousands of words end up in my laptop dustbin.

This is my most personal book yet. It has been twenty years since I started full-time employment in the academy, and so there is something of a consolidation of certain kinds of work I have done over the last two decades, outside of the strictly academic writing I publish in my journal articles and academic book chapters. Some revised chapters bear traces of my earlier writing voices, and I have retained these voices, even though I no longer position myself in that way. On a few occasions, I was struck by a significant political shift in how I had earlier articulated a point than I would now.

I am grateful for the life I have been able to create, that my angels and ancestors have conspired to help me craft, and I am extremely excited about the next two decades of my academic life. I have no desire to write about my life as a broadly autobiographical project. Melinda occasionally tries to check whether I have changed my position on writing a memoir, but my response is always the same, "I will never write a memoir. A few autobiographical essays are as far as I will go." Because she is not just my publisher but has grown into a cherished friend, she knows things she thinks would be interesting to a wider readership. It is not these things I am worried about. It is simply that I aim to take full advantage of having lived my wild twenties before mobile phones had cameras.

Reflecting Rogue: Inside the mind of a feminist contains the musings of one feminist: me. It is an experiment, a risk. All books are. I have revealed parts of myself only known to my nearest and dearest: anxieties, joys, vulnerabilities. I have resisted the urge to make it smoother, and I do not have enough distance yet to know whether it works.

Like all books, the final result differs significantly from the proposed book I sent off to my publisher. I have revealed less about my children than I initially planned to because some of those stories could not just be examples. Their privacy is theirs, as are their stories. As usual, some of the chapters I was most excited about writing have ended up in a draft folder or in the recycling bin. The one I am saddest about is the one dedicated to the humorous misunderstanding between two of my women friends and a recent ex when we were all in our early twenties. Although my friends' passionate but misinformed defence of me always elicits fits of laughter – and occasional horror – when I tell the story at social events, my attempt to tell it on the page was anything but humorous. I'm no Chris van Wyk. Writing is not an exact science, but I try to think it is always worth the trouble.

There were several chapters on rape, femicide and fear that I do not yet feel strong enough to finish and share, so I have left them out. I also know that I will continue to write about violence. However, it is also important that this book not live in the shadow of my previous one, precisely because of the touching success of *Rape: A South African Nightmare*. I have resisted the urge to write an entire book on the Female Fear Factory, even though it seems every week there is more material that tests or expands my thinking on the manufacture of female fear.

I am also still so raw from the violence unleashed on some university campuses in response to #FeesMustFall that I have included nothing in here about the Fallists, except in brief mention in some chapters, and although my position on #RhodesMustFall and #FeesMustFall are both public knowledge, since I have written on it before. I am convinced by the evidence I have seen that a free university education is not only affordable in South Africa, but also one of the best chances we have to significantly change this society into something approximating what we hoped for in 1994. I do not believe the political will exists.

Acknowledgements

I am enormously grateful to my siblings and all my friends who listened to me talk about aspects of this book, gave me their feedback, offered to distract me, or made sure that I had time to write. Its shortcomings are mine. Thank you to Zine Magubane, Reitumetse Mabokela, Jo-Anne Prins, Angelo Fick, Gabeba Baderoon, Nazeema Mohammed and Xolela Mangcu for more insights about insider-outsider status in the academy than I can list, for intellectual generosity and integrity during some really tough battles.

Dina Ligaga, Danai Mupotsa, Sarah Chiumbu and Achieng Ojwang, I marvel at how much you continue to teach me. Grace A Musila, thank you for agreeing to edit another book and for being as frank about what you did not like as you were generous about what works.

Mary Hames, Desiree Lewis, Kudzayi Ngara, Helene Strauss, Nkosinathi Biko, Bruce Walters, Bokang Pooe, Mwelela Cele, Nelleke de Jager for creating avenues for earlier versions of what appear as chapters here. Obenewa Amponsah, you truly are all kinds of magic. I am inspired and tearful with gratitude for you. Three of my favourite chapters in this book would not have happened had it not been for your work.

The people who send me messages, take me on and extend my

other books – especially in the younger generation of queer feminist activists who fill my heart with hope – thank you. My multi-generational feminist community, you are absolutely everything.

To the wonderful #GqolasAngels, you delight, surprise and flatter me and I am so proud of you. I cannot wait to see the appearance of your first books, the day you get your PhDs, those adventures that blow my mind, and I look forward to continuing to see you soar.

Melinda Ferguson, thank you for my three books, for being a writer's dream publisher, a writer's writer and a wonderful friend.

To my sons, Yethu and Vuyani, thank you for choosing to be mine, for spoiling me, challenging me and teaching me. After every book, I swear to both of you that we will now finally have time for all those trips I want to take with you. Well, actually, it will take a lifetime because there are so many, but I can't wait for the next twenty.

Mthetho Tshemese, thank you so much for the wonderful thing you did for my child last year that averted my heart attack. Thank you, Hilda, for knowing all of my madness, for putting me back together when I was a hundred jagged pieces and for your wonderful capacity to hold me accountable while making me feel completely safe.

Bibliography

Adichie CN (accessed 19 May 2014) 'Why can't he just be like anyone else?' *NewswireNGR*. 19 May 2014 http://newswirengr.com/2014/02/19/anti-gay-law-chimamanda-adichie-writes-why-cant-he-just-be-like-everyone-else/#

Adichie, CN (2005) *Purple Hibiscus*, Harper Perennial, New York

Andrade, S (2011) *The nation writ small: African fictions and feminisms, 1958–1988*, Duke University Press, Durham

Andrade, S (1990) 'Rewriting history, motherhood, and rebellion/; naming an African women's literary tradition', *Research in African literatures*, 21 (1), pp. 91–110

Andrade, S (1996) 'The joys of daughterhood: gender, nationalism, and the making of literary tradition(s)', in *Cultural institutions of the novel*, eds, D Lynch and Warner, WB, pp. 249–75, Duke University Press, Durham

Andrade, S (2002) 'Gender and "the public sphere" in Africa: writing women and rioting women', *Agenda* 54, pp. 45–59

Atwood, M (2005) *Curious Pursuits: Occasional Writing*, Virago, London

Awonoor, K (1974) *Guardians of the sacred word*, Nok Publishers, New York

Bâ, M (1981) *So long a letter*, Heinemann, Portsmouth, NH

Baderoon, G (2005) *The dream in the next body*, Kwela, Cape Town

Baderoon, G (accessed 11 March 2010) 'On looking and not looking', *Mail and Guardian*, 09 March http://www.mg.co.za/printformat/single/2010-03-09-on-looking-and-not

Baderoon, G. (2014) *Regarding Muslims: from Slavery to Post-apartheid*, Wits University Press, Johannesburg

Baingana, D (2005) *Tropical Fish*, Kwela, Cape Town

Baingana, D (accessed 10 January 2015), 'The role of offensive language in novels', TEDx Talk, 5 July 2012 https://www.youtube.com/watch?v=zwslzT6DKSI

Berger, J (1972) *Ways of Seeing*, Penguin, London

Bhabha, H (1994) *The location of culture*, Routledge, New York

Busia, APA (1995) 'Fissures in old friendships' in *Moving Beyond Boundaries: International Dimensions in Black Women's Writing* (Volume 1), eds, Davies, CB and Ogundipe-Leslie, M, Pluto, London

Buis, E J (2004) 'Mythology', In *Encyclopedia of Rape*, ed Smith, MD, Greenwood, Westport, CT, pp. 133–4

Buys, A (accessed 18 September 2010) 'My top ten girl artists: the obligatory women's day tribute', *Thought Leader*, 08 August 2010 http://www.thoughtleader.co.za/antheabuys/2008/08/08/my-top-ten-girl-artists-until-august-9-2008-the-obligatory-womens-day-tribute/

Christiansë, Y (accessed 15 March 2010) 'One name came to mind as I read the article in *The Times*: Eudy Simelane' http://book.co.za/blog/2010/03/08/poets-yvette-christianse-and-gabeba-baderoon-respond-to-minister-lulu-xingwana/

Corrigall, M (2009) 'Women themed exhibitions: Aaargh', *The Sunday Independent*, 23 August

Crenshaw, K (1991) 'Mapping the Margins: Intersectionality, Identity Politics and Violence Against Women of Color', *Stanford Law Review* 43, pp. 1241–1279

Dangarembga, T (1988) *Nervous Conditions*, Women's Press, London

Dyson, ME (2004) *The Michael Eric Dyson Reader*, Basic Civitas, New York

Eaton, A W (2003) 'Where ethics and aesthetics meet: Titian's *The Rape of Europa*', *Hypatia: A journal of feminist philosophy*, (184), pp. 159–188

Emecheta, B (1979) *The Joys of Motherhood*, Allison and Busby, London

Evans, S. (accessed 01 March 2010) 'Minister slams 'porn' exhibition', *The Times*, 01 March 2010 http://www.timeslive.co.za/local/article332784.ece

Evans, S (accessed 02 March 2010). 'Xingwana is "conservative" and "reactionary"', *The Times*, 02 March 2010 http://www.timeslive.co.za/local/article334446.ece

Forum for the Empowerment of Women (accessed 15 September 2010) 'FEW is angered by Minister's reaction' http://www.few.org.za/index.php?option=com_content&view=article&id=107:few-is-angered-by-the-ministers-reaction&catid=19:press-release&Itemid=29

Fick, A C (2012) 'Correlations between logic and language: a material history of literacy', Conference paper, Teaching them to read: argument, explanation and logic in undergraduate teaching in South Africa, 1–7 August, University of the Witwatersrand, Johannesburg

Freire, P (2005) [1968] *Pedagogy of the oppressed*, Continuum, London

Gaidzanwa, R (1985) *Images of women in Zimbabwean literature*, College Press, Zimbabwe

Gender DynamiX (accessed 15 September 2010) 'Gender DynamiX speaks out against Xingwana's bigotry' http://www.few.org.za/index.php?option=com_content&view=article&catid=19:press-release&id=105:gender-dynamix-speaks-out-against-xingwanas-bigotry&Itemid=29&layout=default&date=2010-10-01

Gevisser, M (1996) *Potraits of power*, David Philips, Claremont

Gqola, P D (2015) *Rape: a South African nightmare*, MFBooksJoburg/Jacana, Auckland Park

Gqola, P D (2006) 'Re/imagining ways of seeing: making and speaking selves through Zanele Muholi's eyes', in *Only half a picture*, STE, Johannesburg

Gqola, P D (2010) 'Artists are a gift we should treasure', *City Press*, 7 March, pp. 20

Gqola, P D (2013) *A Renegade Called Simphiwe*, MFBookJoburg/Jacana, Auckland Park

Hassim, S (2009) 'Democracy's shadows: sexual rights and gender politics in the rape trial of Jacob Zuma", *African Studies*, 68, (1), pp. 57–77

hooks, b and West, C (1991) *Breaking bread: insurgent Black intellectual life*, South End, New York

Horn, J (accessed 12 June 2014) 'Confronting fundamental sexism in Africa', *Al Jazeera*, 21 May 2014 http://www.aljazeera.com/indepth/opinion/2014/05/confronting-fundamental-sexism-2014520172250423649.html

Jenkins, M (2005) *Breaking the Surface*, Timbila, Elim Hospital

Jordan, J (1980) *Passion: new poems, 1977–1980*, Beacon Press, Boston

Katrak K H (1995) 'Decolonising culture: Toward a theory for post-colonial women's texts', in *The Post Colonial Studies Reader*, eds, Ashcroft, B, Griffiths, G and Tiffin, H, Routledge, New York

Kay, J (1990) *Adoption papers*, Bloodaxe, New Castle

Kaul, S (1996) 'Colonial Figures and Postcolonial Reading", *Diacritics*. 26 (1)

Khusi, P D (2002) 'An Afrocentric Approach to Tertiary Education in South Africa: Personal Reflections', in *Discourses on Difference, Discourses on Oppression*, eds, Duncan, N, Gqola, PD, Hofmeyr, M, Shefer, T, Malunga, F, and Mashige, M, Centre for Advanced Studies of African Society, Cape Town

Landry, D and Maclean, G (1996) (eds) *The Spivak Reader*, Routledge, New York

Legum, Margaret. (Accessed 20 December 2016) 'I was a white liberal and survived', *Mail and Guardian*. 15 March 1996 https://mg.co.za/article/1996-03-15-i-was-a-white-liberal-and-survived/

Lewis, D (1992) 'Myths of motherhood and power: the construction of "Black woman" in literature', *English in Africa*, 19 (1), pp. 35–51

Lorde, A (1984) *Sister Outsider*, Crossing Press, Berkley

Mabokela, RO (2000) *Voices of Conflict: Desegregating South African Universities*, Routledge Falmer, New York

Mabokela, R O and King, K L (2001) (eds) *Apartheid No More: Case Studies of Southern African Universities in the Process of Transformation*, Bergin and Garvey, Westport, CT

Mabokela, R O and Magubane, Z (2003) (eds) *Race, Gender and the Status of Black South African Women in the Academy*, UNISA Press, Pretoria

Maldonado-Torres, N (2008) *Against war: views from the underside of modernity*, Duke University Press, Durham

Mbembe, A (2001) *On the postcolony*, University of California Press, Oakland, CA

McFadden, P (2003) 'Sexual Pleasure as Feminist Choice', *Feminist Africa* (2), http://agi.ac.za/sites/agi.ac.za/files/fa_2_standpoint_1.pdf

McKaiser, E (accessed 15 March 2010) 'Minister's attitude is not only dangerous, it's also deadly, *Daily Dispatch*, 08 March http://www.dispatch.co.za/article.aspx?id=385618

Mulvey, L (1975) 'Visual pleasure and narrative cinema', *Screen*, 16 (3), pp. 6–18

Mulvey, L (1989) *Visual and Other Pleasures*, Indiana University Press, Bloomington, IN

Mda, L (1996) 'The Truth about ReCONciliation: It's con', *Tribute*, December

Momple, L (2001) *Neighbours: the story of a murder*, Heinemann, Portsmouth, NH

Motsemme, N and Ratele, K (2002) 'Losing life and re-making nation:

the Truth and Reconciliation Commission', in *Discourses on difference, discourses on oppression,* eds, N Duncan, Gqola, PD, Hofmeyr, M, Shefer, T, Malunga, F and Mashige, M, pp. 307–330, CASAS, Plumstead

Moudileno, L (2015) 'The troubling popularity of West African romance novels', *Research in African Literatures,* 39 (4), pp. 120–32

Mupotsa, D (accessed 21 August 2009) 'Lobola for my love', *Mail and Guardian,* 23 July 2008 https://mg.co.za/article/2008-07-18-lobola-for-my-love

Mupotsa, D (2015) 'The promise of happiness: desire, attachment and freedom in post/apartheid South Africa', *Critical Arts* 29 (2), pp. 183–98

Mupotsa, D (2014) *White weddings,* Doctoral dissertation, University of the Witwatersrand, Johannesburg

Musila, GA (2009) 'Phallocracies and gynocratic transgressions: gender, state power and Kenyan public life', *Africa Insight,* 39 (1), pp. 39–57

Mwangi, W (accessed 10 December 2013) 'Silence is a woman', *New Inquiry,* 4 June 2013 https://thenewinquiry.com/silence-is-a-woman/

Ndashe, S (accessed 11 May 2006) 'Can I speak, please?' *Pamabazuka: weekly forum for social justice in Africa.* http://www.pambazuka.org/en/category/comment/34138 reprinted in *Grace, Tenacity and Eloquence: the struggle for women's rights in Africa,* eds, Burnett, P, Karmali, S Manji, F, Fahamu, Nairobi, pp. 171–173

Ndebele, N (2007) *Fine Lines from the Box: Further thoughts about our country,* Umuzi, Houghton

Ndebele, N (2006) [1990] *Rediscovery of the Ordinary: Essays on South African literature and culture,* UKZN Press, Scottsville

Nnaemeka 0 (1998 (ed), *Sisterhood, feminism and power: from Africa to the Diaspora,* Africa World Press, Trenton, NJ

Nwapa, F (1966) *Efuru,* Heinemann, Portsmouth

Ogundipe-Leslie, M (1994) *Recreating Ourselves: African women and critical transformations,* Africa World Press, Trenton, NJ

Ogundipe-Leslie, M (2001) 'Moving the mountains, making the links', in *Feminism & 'Race',* ed, Bhavnani, K, Oxford University Press, New York

Ogunyemi, CO (2009) 'Prolepsis: Twelve telling tales by African women', in *Twelve Best Books by African Women: Critical Reflections,* eds. Ogunyemi, CO and Allan, TJ, pp. 1–13, University of Ohio Press, Athens, OH

Ogunyemi, CO (1985) 'Womanism: The dynamics of the contemporary black female novel in English' in *Signs: Journal of Women in Culture and Society* 11 (1), pp. 63–80

Oppelt, P (accessed 9 March 2010) "Take off the blinkers, minister", *The Times*, 08 March 2010 http://www.timeslive.co.za/opinion/columnists/article344785.ece/Take-off-the-blinkers-minister

Orr, M (2003) *Intertextuality: Debates and contexts*, Polity, Cambridge

O'Toole, S (accessed 18 September 2010) 'Return of the Censors', *Mahala*, 4 March, Available at http://www.mahala.co.za/art/return-of-the-censors/

Perumal, V (2007) *Identity, Diversity and Teaching for Social Justice*, Peter Lang, Berlin

Phillips, L and McCaskill, B (1995) 'Who's schooling who? Black women and bringing the everyday into the academe, or why we founded *The Womanist*', *Signs* 20 (4), pp. 1007–1018

Pillay, V (accessed 04 March 2010) 'Xingwana: But is it art?', *Mail and Guardian*, 04 March 2010 http://www.mg.co.za/article/2010-03-04-xingwana-but-is-it-art

Qunta, C (1998) 'From Other to Us', *Tribute*, April

Ratele, K (2016) *Liberating masculinities*, HSRC Press, Cape Town

Rushie, S (1988) *Satanic Verses*, Viking, New York

Said, E (1983). 'Traveling theory', *The world, the text, and the critic*. Harvard University Press, Cambridge, MA, pp. 226–47

Salo, E (2005) 'Multiple targets, mixing strategies: complicating feminist analysis of South African women's movements', *Feminist Africa* (4), pp. 64–71

Salo, E (2003) 'Negotiating gender and personhood in the New South Africa', *European Journal of Cultural Studies*, 6 (3), pp. 345–365

Shange, N (2010) [1975] *for colored girls who have considered suicide/ when the rainbow is enuf*, Scribner, New York

Smith, G (2010) 'Minister shoots self in foot', *City Press*, 7 March

Stone, D (1972) 'The source of Titian's *The Rape of Europa*', *The Art Bulletin*, 54 (1), pp. 47–49

Spencer, L (2014) *Writing Women in Uganda and South Africa: Emerging from Post-Repressive Regimes* Doctoral dissertation, Stellenbosch University, Stellenbosch

Spencer, L (2016) 'Abagyenda bareeba. Those who Travel, See': Home, Migration and the Maternal Bond in Doreen Baingana's *Tropical Fish*', *African Studies* 75 (2), pp. 189–201

Spivak, GC (1996). 'Bonding in Difference' (with Alfred Arteaga), in *The Spivak Reader*, eds, Landry, D and Maclean, G, Routledge, New York

Spivak, GC (1990) 'The post-colonial critic', in *The Post-colonial Critic: Interviews, Strategies, Dialogues,* ed, Harasym, S, Routledge, London

Steyn, M and van Zyl, M (2009) *The Prize and the Price: Shaping sexualities in South Africa,* HSRC

Sturken, M (1998) 'The remembering of forgetting: recovered memory and the question of experience', *Social Text* 16 (4), pp. 103–25

Swanson, D (1949) *Jim comes to Jo'burg,* Film, MNet

Van Wyk, Chris (2004) *Shirley, Goodness and Mercy,* Picador, Johannesburg

Wainaina, B (2011) *One day I will write about this place,* Kwani, Nairobi

Walker, A (1982) *The Color Purple,* Women's Press, London

Walker, A (1985) *In Search of our Mothers' Gardens: Womanist prose,* Women's Press, London

Walker, A (1992) *Possessing the secret of joy,* Pocket, New York

Walker, A (2000) *The way forward is with a broken heart,* Ballantine, New York

Wicomb, Z (2000) *David's Story,* Kwela, Cape Town

Williams, P J (1991) *The alchemy of race and rights: The diary of a law professor,* Harvard University Press, Cambridge, MA

Wintle, M (2004). *Europa and the Bull, Europe, and European Studies: Visual images as historical source materials,* Vossiurspers UvAX, Amsterdam